WOMEN ON THE SPECTRUM

A HANDBOOK FOR LIFE

DR. EMMA GOODALL
YENN PURKIS

AAPC PUBLISHING
©2020

Your First Source for Practical Solutions for Autism Spectrum and Related Disorders

Exceptional Resources For Extraordinary Minds

AAPC PUBLISHING
PO Box 861116
Shawnee, KS 66216

Local Phone (913) 897-1004 Fax (913) 728-6090

www.aapcpublishing.com

Copyright © 2020 by AAPC Publishing

Printed in the United States of America

Names: Goodall, Emma, 1971- author. | Purkis, Jeanette, 1974- author.

Title: Women on the spectrum : a handbook for life / Dr. Emma Goodall, Jeanette "Yenn" Purkis.

Description: Shawnee, KS : AAPC Publishing, [2020] | Audience: Adolescent and adult women on the autism spectrum.

Identifiers: ISBN: 9781942197577 (paperback) | 9781942197584 (kindle)

Subjects: LCSH: Autistic people--Life skills guides. | Autistic girls--Life skills guides. | Young women with disabilities--Life skills guides. | Women with mental disabilities--Life skills guides. | Autism spectrum disorders--Patients--Life skills guides. | Asperger's syndrome--Patients--Life skills guides. | Autistic girls--Education. | Autistic people--Social life and customs. | Autistic people--Family relationships. | Autistic people--Sexual behavior. | Parents with mental disabilities--Life skills guides.

Classification: LCC: RC553.A88 G657 2020 | DDC: 616.85/882--dc23

TABLE OF CONTENTS

INTRODUCTION

DR. EMMA GOODALL

This is not the book I set out to write. However, it is the book that I wrote after I decided that the chapters previously written would not actually enable girls and women on the autism spectrum to most effectively learn from my and others' mistakes! As a female with a diagnosis of Aspergers, I have referred to myself as an aspie, but as a self-advocate in the Autism Self Advocacy Network of Australia, New Zealand and Oceania, I refer to myself as autistic. In my professional life I use identity first language unless an organisation has policies that require person first. In both cases I refuse to use the D from ASD or the word disorder, as 'dis ' order doesn't seem to describe us autistics very well.

YENN PURKIS

Emma invited me to co-author this book in mid-2017. I thought it would be such a valuable resource for autistic women and girls that I agreed with no hesitation. As an autistic woman there are a number of things I have learned through varying degrees of challenge and difficulty. It makes sense for me to co-author this book which uses Emma and my experience and knowledge to help other autistic women to navigate life more effectively, address challenges and to avoid trauma and invalidation where they can. In this book the word autistic will be used to describe children, young people and adults who are "on" the autism spectrum whether with a formal diagnosis or not. The term 'autistic', in this book will cover autism, Aspergers and the autism spectrum. The word girl will be used to describe children and young people who identify or are self-identified as female. In the same way, the word woman will be used to reference adults who are identified as, or who self-identify as female. Much of the information presented could be equally applied to other children, young people and adults who are autistic.

Over the last year, a large number of women have asked us to include a number of topics in this book so that they can get the explicit answers to a range of questions about growing up, navigating adult life and growing old well, as autistic girls and women.

Whilst in hospital, struggling with health complications that had been missed due to communication issues arising from her autistic communication style, Emma came to a realization about the book: An advice and guidance or Question and Answer format would be the most useful approach for this book.

This book Is structured as chapters covering broad topics with questions from autistic women and answers addressing the issues raised in the questions. It will enable readers to dip in and out, getting the information they most need when they most want it, rather than having to read a whole chapter to find an answer or at least part of an answer.

---

[1] Identity first language examples: 'autistic', 'aspie' Person first language examples: 'child on the autism spectrum', 'adult with a diagnosis of autism'

GETTING TO KNOW YOURSELF

WHAT DOES YOUR AUTISM MEAN FOR YOU?

Question:

What are the typical 'female autistic spectrum characteristics and behaviors'?

Advice and Guidance:

It should be noted that gender is not binary and people identify their gender differently so identifying specific gendered characteristics needs to be considered within that context. Also, some male autistics have the characteristics considered more 'female' and vice versa. The idea of gendered characteristics has value its some cases, but it is often more confusing than enlightening and each individual autistic person experiences gender and autism differently, bearing this in mind, some of the characteristics of autism traditionally viewed as 'female' include:

▶ Masking, acting or being a social chameleon. They can come at the cost of a sense of identity, and exhaustion but people engage in masking to be seen as more socially acceptable. This highlights a skill in copying or mimicry rather than an innate understanding of how to 'be' in different contexts.

- Interest in nature, animals and the environment as well as a strong bond with animals
- Deep sensory abilities, highly intuitive
- Hyper empathy (i.e. feeling what another person is feeling just by being physically close to them)
- Interest in things like philosophy and spirituality
- A strong sense of social justice
- More of a focus on creative activities like art, music and writing
- A strong interest in helping others
- Can be quite interested in socializing and friends
- Often hold everything together so at school they are the quiet girl up the back but when they get home they may have a meltdown or shutdowns after masking all day long at school

Question:

How do I explain my daughter/my partner's sensory issues to my family or other people?

Advice and Guidance:

Sensory issues are very common among autistic people but rarely experienced by non-autistic people. The main sticking point around understanding sensory issues is often based on that level of different experience. A sound which is barely noticed by the non-autistic person may be excruciatingly loud and offensive to an autistic person with sensory sensitivities. It is not the case that the non-autistic person is being deliberately difficult or the autistic person being overly sensitive. A lack of understanding of sensory issues may well be due to an inability by the non-autistic person to relate to something outside of their lived experience.

It can be difficult to bridge that experience gap but that is often the best way to start to develop understanding. One way to explain sensory processing issues is to give the person who does not have sensory issues the example of the kind of extreme sensory input that autistic people can experience. For example, toothpaste can be replaced with wasabi or chilli. Hand dryers or construction noise compared to a plane taking off right by your house, and the feel of clothes on the skin – or labels on clothing – with coarse sandpaper. You can explain to the person that there is a difference, much like a cat or dog hears and sees on different wavelengths. Explain that just because it isn't a shared experience does not mean it isn't real.

In the workplace sensory difficulties can result in a person becoming highly stressed, which activates noradrenaline/norepinephrine, the brain chemical responsible for sympathetic nervous system overload (SNS overload). SNS overload results in human survival instinct kicking in, and the thinking part of the brain shutting down to enable the most energy efficient fight/flight/freeze of the body, maximizing the likelihood of survival. What this survival instinct looks like from the outside are behaviours commonly described in autistics as meltdowns or shutdowns.

In the workplace, no autistic employee wants to have a meltdown, or even a shutdown (which is more socially acceptable). Even if they don't result in SNS overload, unaddressed sensory challenges can result in poor performance and disengagement of an employee who would otherwise be a high performer. Some people have left workplaces or sold their home because of sensory issues. Modifications to support a comfortable sensory environment include things like; removing the fluorescent light bulbs from over your desk, wearing sunglasses or a hat, wearing headphones, having a fragrance free area in the office, using a standing desk or sitting on a swiss ball rather than an office chair.

Just because somebody else doesn't experience the same reactions sensory input as you, does not mean you are overreacting or that you shouldn't have the problem distressing sensory experiences addressed.

Question:

Why don't I/my daughter/my partner understand instructions?

Advice and Guidance:

When instructions are spoken, many autistics can struggle to follow them if they consist of many parts. Instructions are said to be; single step, two step, three step or multi-step. Single step instructions contain one phrase, for example sit here, whereas two step instructions will contain two phrases, such as get your book and sit here. Three step instructions, such as, get your book, open it to page four and read the first paragraph, have three steps. Multi-step instructions contain more than three instructions.

Many autistics, and some non-autistics, have some level of auditory processing disorder that means they process speech more slowly than other people. When you are processing each chunk of speech in your brain, this processing turns sounds into electrical signals via the ear and then into understandable concepts in the brain. Only then can you follow the instructions. For some autistics, it can take 30-60 seconds to process each phrase, which can lead to a sort of traffic jam of electrical signals from the ear to the sense making part of the brain. When this happens, if instructions are more than a single step, the person often appears to only 'hear' the first or last step of the instruction. Whereas, it is not the hearing, it is the slower sense making that is an issue.

If you or someone you know has difficulty following instructions, try giving/receiving instructions in a single step format. This means each phrase is spoken and the next one not spoken until the person has already followed the initial or preceding instruction. Many people assume incompetence where auditory processing difficulties are the real culprit.

You can test your auditory processing difficulties by getting someone to give you instructions in the different step formats and with no, 5 second, 10 second, 20 second, 30 second and longer processing times. An alternative is to ask for an assessment with a speech and language therapist, which may have a wait period and a cost associated with it.

Question:

What do people mean when they say my social skills aren't very good?

Advice and Guidance:

The idea of 'good social skills' is usually based on the idea that the kinds of social communication and interaction that non-autistic people have is the 'correct' way and any deviation from that is 'incorrect.'

Non-autistic people have a distinctly different style of

social communication to autistic people. They tend to use more levels of meaning so that the words they say might not be what they mean. Non-autistic communication relies on a lot of non-verbal cues and body language such as eye contact, much more than autistic communication does. There are a range of hidden or 'unwritten rules' in non-autistic communication which can be confusing to the autistic person. These are sometimes described as a hidden curriculum and there are some helpful resources about learning the hidden curriculum for a given area.

As non-autistic people are in the majority in society, anyone whose communication is different to that supposed 'norm' is likely to be considered unusual. Their social skills can be called into question. A lot of the focus on services for autistic children is based on teaching them 'good social skills'. There can be some value in this up to a point: being able to speak the 'language' of the non-autistic majority is certainly useful on occasion. However, the notion of 'good' non-autistic social skills and 'poor' autistic ones is quite problematic. For example, in the situation of a schoolyard bully who is harassing an autistic child, often the social skills training will be directed at the autistic child. But whose social skills are more in need of addressing? Surely the bully is expressing far worse social behaviour than their autistic victim?

So basically when someone says an autistic person's social skills are poor, it tends to come from the position that neurotypical = good socially and autistic = poor socially, which is not particularly helpful. Autistic and non-autistic communication can be seen simply as different languages. While it is useful to speak the other language, it does not mean one is better than the other.

In addition, there has been the idea that having 'good' social skills will enable us to make and keep friends, however research indicates that this is not the case.

Rather, having opportunities to interact with people interested in a shared interest area is the most likely pathway to making and keeping friends.

Question:

How can I develop my/my daughter/my partner's emotional regulation?

Advice and Guidance:

Emotional regulation is a part of self-awareness and insight. Autistic people can really struggle with this, often because they have a condition called Alexithymia. This is sometimes called emotion blindness. It does not mean that a person has no emotions. Rather it relates to a difficulty or inability to articulate and be aware of one's emotions. It is not exclusive to autistic people but is significantly more common among autistic people.

In addition many autistics have atypical interoception, which is the sense of your internal self. For example interoception, otherwise known as interoceptive awareness, enables you to know when you are hot or cold and to do something about it. It is thought that there is a strong link between poor interoception and alexithymia.

One of the ways both alexithymia and atypical interoception can impact you is that you would only know that you are experiencing an emotion when it is at a very high level. It may look like a person goes from zero to 100 (emotions-wise) whereas in fact the emotion was going on the whole time - they just weren't aware of it. Much of the resulting behaviours are actually due to SNS overload, but are often misunderstood as challenging behaviour. Long terms alexithymia and/or atypical interoception can lead to mental health difficulties. In addition for some people with alexithymia and/or atypical interoception, mental illness conditions such as borderline personality disorder can be misattributed due to their atypical body language and responses to their environment and life situations.

People with alexithymia can learn to regulate their emotions but it may take some practice and time. One strategy is to make a list of what happens in the lead-up to an extreme of emotions. For example, when you are depressed you might stop cleaning your home or wanting to get out of bed and when you are anxious you might talk about the thing you are anxious about a lot more frequently. Next time you notice yourself doing these actions you will have a heads-up on what your mood is doing which can help you take measures to address it.

In addition, if you have atypical interoception you improve this through regularly doing interoception activities where you are consciously noticing changes in your body. Some examples of these can be found in a creative commons interoception curriculum from the Department for Education and Child Development in South Australia:

http://web.seru.sa.edu.au/wp-content/uploads/2019/04/Interoception-101_March-2019.pdf

http://web.seru.sa.edu.au/wp-content/uploads/2019/04/Interoception-201_March-2019.pdf

http://web.seru.sa.edu.au/wp-content/uploads/2017/09/sensory-overview.pdf

There are a number of skills you can use to support emotion regulation. These include:

▸ Improving your interoceptive awareness and accuracy by changing your body state and actively noticing where you feel that change and what the change feels like. Over time you will start to be aware of how your body feels when it is signalling that you are experiencing different emotions, and then you can respond to them in a timely manner.

- ▶ Distraction. This skill involves focusing your attention on something other than your mood. An activity you enjoy is usually a good place to start. This is a way of distracting yourself from the emotional distress. It probably won't 'fix' it but it will keep you in a less unpleasant place and can give you some relief from extreme emotions. You may need to practice distraction a number of times a day if you are experiencing a lot of emotional distress, but be aware this kind of distress does not last forever and will pass. Interoception activities act as both a physical and biological distracter when in emotional distress as they often lower your heart rate, which is a signal that the parasympathetic nervous system has been activated (rest and digest) and that the SNS is no longer in control.

- ▶ Opposite action. This skill involves doing the opposite of what your brain and negative emotions are telling you to do. It can work very effectively against depression. It seems to work by using the opposite action to sort of trick the brain into thinking it is happier. Some nice practical applications include if you don't feel like getting out of bed, because you are feeling depressed or sad or unmotivated, then get out of bed and have a shower or if you feel you can't do the dishes or vacuuming then do it. It is unlikely to be easy, particularly at first, but it can be very effective.

- ▶ Some people benefit from mindfulness meditation to help them build awareness of their emotions and manage distress.

Question:

Can I self-advocate for changes to work or class/ school without disclosure of an autism spectrum diagnosis, or if I don't yet have a diagnosis?

Advice and Guidance:

While it is usually a lot easier to advocate for change if you do have a diagnosis, it is also possible to advocate without sharing your diagnosis, or even if you do not have a formal diagnosis. This kind of advocacy basically involves explaining the specific challenges you are facing and how they impact on you and requesting action be taken to support you or to address your difficulty. It is preferable to clearly state what happens or what will happen if your request is not granted. For example,"if I have to work in fluorescent or LED lights I will find it a lot harder to do my work. This is due to a sensory issue I have which magnifies the light from LEDs and fluorescents to a point where I find it almost impossible to concentrate enough to do my work. It also means that due to being stressed and uncomfortable, I will find it harder to communicate effectively with my colleagues". Then you can explain the change which needs to be made to accommodate your needs. In the example above that might mean removing the offending lights and giving the person a lamp to use at her desk.

However, while it is possible to advocate for yourself without a diagnosis / disclosure, it can be a lot harder. This is simply due to how Western society and institutions like school and workplaces approach medical diagnoses. If you say to your employer "I am autistic" they are more likely to accommodate your needs because autism is a known condition and there is a legal requirement to make accommodations in many countries via disability discrimination laws or equal opportunity legislation. If you are having difficulties accessing support and adjustments it might be worth considering seeking a formal diagnosis or talking to your employer or school about your diagnosis if you have one.

Question:

What is the difference between a shutdown and a meltdown and why do they happen?

Advice and Guidance:

Both meltdowns and shutdowns are something which autistic people experience when they are in SNS overload. Overload can relate to social, emotional, sensory or other difficulties or often a combination of these. The neurotransmitter noradrenaline/norepinephrine signals stress or other negative emotions/states to the brain and continues to build the danger signal until either the perceived danger has been addressed or the SNS goes into overload to activate our survival instinct; fight, flight or freeze.

A meltdown occurs when the survival instinct is expressed via fight/flight, whereas a shutdown occurs when it is expressed as freeze (or flop/drop). People do not choose to have a meltdown or shutdown. Indeed, SNS overload PREVENTS the thinking parts of the brain from working so the person CANNOT make any choices at that moment in time. This is why approaching a child in meltdown who is running away and trying to hold them (even if this is to try and keep them safe) usually ends up with the child trying to hurt the 'helper'. The child is expressing their SNS overload through the survival instinct of flight and their brain is focused on surviving perceived danger and cannot think, thus the approaching person is perceived as dangerous and so the survival behaviour needs to be upped to ensure survival.

Meltdowns (externalizing survival behaviours) and shutdowns (internalizing survival behaviours) are not deliberate and usually the person who wishes it hadn't happened the most is the person experiencing this. Meltdowns are often misunderstood, sometimes being interpreted as tantrums where the person is deliberately 'acting out' in order to get their own way, or simply poor behaviour and / or a lack of control. A meltdown or shutdown can be understood a bit like a release valve, once the brain has 'ensured survival of the body' the body can be in control again.

However, it is always preferable to be aware when SNS stress is happening which unless dealt with will always end in a meltdown or shutdown. When SNS stress is building, de-escalation strategies can prevent SNS overload by chemically signaling to the SNS that the danger/issue has passed and activating the parasympathetic nervous system.

In our current world, meltdowns can be quite dangerous for those people experiencing them. A number of autistic people have been tragically killed by law enforcement officers, who lacking adequate training and understanding of autism and meltdowns, have assumed the person was a danger to others. In some cases, autistic adults, often lacking an official autism diagnosis, have spent years as involuntary patients in locked psychiatric wards due to their meltdowns being misunderstood as wilful 'bad behaviour' and the hospital environment making matters worse.

Anecdotally, autistic women seem to experience shutdowns of a long duration in response to long term stress. Shutdowns can look similar to depression or be accompanied by depression. If you think this describes you, you may benefit from stress reduction strategies such as yoga, pilates, mindfulness, making and spending time with friends (whether online or in real life). Having even just one positive interpersonal relationship is known to be the biggest single protective factor against depression and anything that helps to reduce stress can help to prevent shutdowns.

Question:

What does it mean when a diagnosis report says that someone has 'poor executive functioning'?

Advice and Guidance:

Executive functioning is an area in which autistic people often have difficulties that impact on their life in a variety of ways. The official definition of executive functioning is:

> *The executive functions are a set of processes that all have to do with managing oneself and one's resources in order to achieve a goal. It is an umbrella term for the neurologically-based skills involving mental control and self-regulation.* [2]

Difficulties with executive function are often viewed as being disorganised but executive functioning captures a range of areas, including:

▸ The ability to move freely from one situation to another and to think flexibly in order to respond appropriately to the situation.

▸ The ability to stop one's own behaviour at the appropriate time, The ability to modulate emotional responses

[2]http://www.ldonline.org/article/29122/ accessed 21 December 2017

- The ability to begin a task or activity and to independently generate ideas, responses, or problem-solving strategies.
- The capacity to hold information in mind for the purpose of completing a task
- The ability to monitor one's own performance and to measure it against some standard of what is needed or expected
- Planning and organisation[3]

Autistic people and those with some other neurodivergent conditions such as ADHD can have difficulties with executive functioning. It is not your 'fault' if you have these difficulties. Your capacity for executive functioning is hard-wired into your brain. Previously, it was thought that it was not possible to change neural pathways affecting executive function, so that it was assumed that if you have a difficulty in that area you will always have an issue there. However, it is possible that with developing neuroplasticity research this will change. In the meantime, there are a number of practical strategies that you can use to maximize your executive functioning. Most people use planners or diaries, whether written down or electronic. Planners and diaries are simple tools to support the planning and time management aspects of executive functioning.

The best way to approach executive functioning issues is to find a 'workaround' for each issue and to put in place in strategies in areas where you struggle. Some people make good use of lists and calendars and notices stuck up at home or in the office. Other people find that bullet journals are more helpful for them than alarm reminders on their phones. If you have difficulties with motor planning (moving your body how you want it to move) you may find sessions with an occupational therapist useful or you may find yoga

[3]http://www.ldonline.org/article/29122/ accessed 21 December 2017

or interoception activities useful, or you may choose to walk or drive rather than use a bicycle!

Both the authors of this book have issues with geography and directions but we have put in place a number of strategies to address this. These kinds of strategies are often unique to the individual and they are something you can refine and perfect over time. For example, using a transport app can help you to work out how to get from one place to another.

Having executive functioning issues does not mean you will never be able to do the things you struggle with but it does mean you will need to devise some handy strategies to manage your difficulties with those things. A simple strategy that can be used for people who struggle with directions is to hold your hands up in front of your face, palms facing away and thumbs stretched out. The left hand makes a capital L in this position and so you can then tell reliably which is YOUR left and YOUR right. You can also use your way and my way if you are driving or walking with someone else!

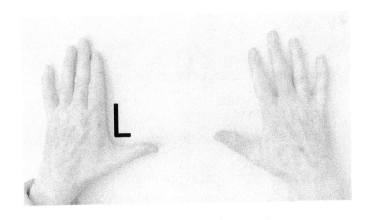

Question:

Do autistic women often have autistic friends? What are the advantages of friendship with others on the autism spectrum?

Advice and Guidance:

Autistic people – men and women – often have autistic friends. There are some very clear reasons for this. If you see autism as being a culture with its own language and shared experiences then having autistic friends can be compared with an expatriate living in a country with a very different language and culture. While the expatriate can speak the language of their new home, it is usually easier for them to mix with other expatriates from their own country and culture and language, as they do not have to navigate a second (or third) language to interact with others. Many autistics talking about 'finding my tribe' which refers to their autistic peer group but also the sort of autistic cultural experience that comes along with that.

Some of the advantages of having friends on the autism spectrum include:

- ▸ The likelihood of shared experiences, strengths and support needs, with other autistic women
- ▸ Talking the same language – i.e. communicating in an autistic way
- ▸ Autistics are generally very honest and loyal friends
- ▸ Possibility of mutual support
- ▸ Significantly lower likelihood of being patronized or discriminated against
- ▸ Lower likelihood of a power imbalance in the friendship (although this can happen between au-

tistic friends too)

- ▶ More likelihood of being understood and being able to be yourself around your friends without fear or being rejected or being perceived as weird.

It is important to note that good friends, whether or not they are also autistic, will accept and value you because of who you are and not in spite of who you are.

Question:

Even though I have a diagnosis I am finding it really difficult to accept I am on the autism spectrum. What can I do?

Advice and Guidance:

While a lot of adult women respond to their diagnosis as a liberation and a welcome revelation, not everyone does. For some women the diagnosis results in mixed feelings. Some people flatly refuse to accept their diagnosis. Given that autistic women are under-diagnosed and there are a lot of stereotypes about what autism 'looks like', it can be very challenging for women to see themselves as part of the autistic community if they don't fit the picture in their mind of what autism is. For some women their difficulty accepting their diagnosis relates to low self-esteem and/or seeing the diagnosis in purely negative terms.

Some strategies to help you learn to accept and like your diagnosis include:

- ▶ Reflect on why you are struggling to accept your diagnosis. Are you struggling to accept a diagnosis that is seen negatively by many people or that you perceive as being negative? You can talk it over with trusted friends and / or family if you like. Knowing the cause of your difficulty accepting your diagnosis is a good way to start addressing it. You probably won't figure it out the first time you think about it but it is a good way to start coming to terms with it.

- ▸ Meet some other autistic women. You can go to a face-to-face support group or join some autistic women's groups online. If you know any autistic women in your life - at work or your children's school etc., and they seem approachable you might want to start up a conversation with them if they are happy to chat.

- ▸ Look at some blogs or books written by autistic women. This can help you to relate autistic women's experiences to your own. Most resources by autistic women are affirming and positive about their own and others' autistic identity. If you find one of the first things you read to be at odds with your experiences or truly annoying, it is ok to put that down (or in my case throw it across the room), but you will find that there really is a wide range of experiences out there and it is likely that you will identify with at least one, so persist in reading or watching videos by autistic women.

- ▸ Do some research on women and autism. You could look at well-known and / or notable autistic women. This will hopefully give you some idea of what autistic women are like and what they can achieve and how they rarely fit the stereotypes.

- ▸ Of course, all these strategies are based on the assumption that you actually wish to accept your diagnosis. If you are struggling with even the idea of it applying to you, it may take some time to get into a space where you can think about it in terms of acceptance. This is OK too. Acceptance is not a race.

Question:

Since I was a young girl I have found it easiest to just mimic what others were doing in order to be accepted by other people but now I am not 100 percent sure of what my actual identity is. Is this common for autistic women?

Advice and Guidance:

Acting, masking and mimicking are a way of navigating the non-autistic world which a lot of autistics use. This serves a purpose of feeling able to be accepted socially by non-autistic people, but it can have a really unpleasant consequence of the person doing it losing all sense of who they are.

Acting and masking tends it be used by people who are afraid of discrimination and bullying, or desperate to fit in and be accepted by those around them. It's not 'wrong' to do it but it is helpful to be aware it is happening. It takes some autistic women years to reclaim their identity. We all have the right to our identity and the amount of acting that goes on is representative of a society which is not respectful of our differences.

Some autistic women with similar experiences have taken it as an opportunity to consciously build their character and identity. If you can do this there are a lot of advantages. One of the most difficult things with being a social chameleon is that you don't know whether others like and respect you or the character you are showing them. This can be addressed by getting in touch with other autistic people who may share your experience of masking and acting. These people are likely to understand your situation and are likely to give you honest feedback as well as support.

Some non-autistic people see people masking and think they are being deliberately dishonest and they appear noticeably different in different settings. For the person masking that can be incredibly hurtful. Masking and acting are not deliberate dishonesty at all. They are a means of survival in an often confusing and hostile world. Masking and acting really need to be understood more broadly as the accusations of dishonesty against autistic people who tend to be significantly more honest than most is something which needs to stop.

Question:

I am trans and identify as female. Are there a lot of trans people who are also autistic?

Advice and Guidance:

A large number of autistic people are trans, gender fluid, non-binary and gender Queer. Emerging research suggests that a much greater proportion of autistic people are non-binary gender, trans and / or gender fluid. It is not yet clear why this might be the case, with some people suggesting a neurological connection. Others suggest that autistic people are divergent in other domains anyway and so are more likely to be conformable with their actual gender identity, as opposed to neurotypical people, who may struggle with accepting their gender diversity due to being more socially conforming. There are a great many trans autistics. If you want to meet other autistic trans women, there are groups online you can join. You are far from alone.

Question:

A lot of the material on autism and gender I have seen is based in cis gender / born as female women. How do the sort of female autism traits work when someone is trans or non-binary gender?

Advice and Guidance:

As described above, the notion of 'gendered' autism types is actually quite fraught and unhelpful. Gender goes way beyond just male and female. It could be said that there are as many distinct genders as there are human beings. So attaching attributes to autistic people based on the binary notion of 'male autism traits' and 'female autism traits' is not particularly useful. If you are trans of gender fluid or non-binary, how do you know which gendered autism 'type' describes you?

It is preferable to qualify the notion of female and male autism traits with that understanding in mind. There may be some value in holding onto notions of gendered autism traits when diagnosing adult women, for example, but as an absolute or template it is unhelpful and likely to cause confusion.

There are also some really unhelpful notions of gender and autism such as the now largely discredited 'extreme male brain' theory. A more nuanced understanding of gender and autism essentially leads to understanding that the absolutes and 'either / or' views do not really stack up against the evidence and experience of autistic people. For some trans women autistics they present their autism in typically female ways, whilst some cis male autistics (born male) also present their autism with these characteristics.

EARLY CHILDHOOD

EFFECTIVE PARENTING OF AUTISTIC SPECTRUM GIRLS

Much of this chapter applies to both female, male and intersex babies and toddlers who may be on the autism spectrum. All of the strategies in this chapter are useful whether or not the child does turn out to be autistic or not. However, they are written with the autistic mindset and autistic characteristics at the forefront.

Question:

I am worried about breastfeeding, because I think it may be a sensory problem for me as I am autistic.

Advice and Guidance:

Medical research indicates that 'breast is best' (REF), but it is important to accept that not all mothers can breastfeed whether or not they are the biological birth mother or any other kind of parent. If it is at all possible to use the birth mother's breast milk for the baby by using a breast pump where breastfeeding is not possible this is a great solution. If not, it is about sourcing high quality powdered milk.

The issues with breastfeeding for autistic mums and babies are multiple and are briefly described here as many mums, whether or not they are autistic, can feel that they are the only person going through what they are currently experiencing:

- Very little breast milk...
- Sore/cracked nipples....
- Baby struggles to 'latch' on
- Baby struggles to 'suck' effectively
- Baby/mum dislikes the whole thing...Sensory stuff
- Baby vomits after every breastfeed — I was apparently one of these babies and my mother struggled to breast feed me through my and then her growing distress as I vomited after every feed. Her brilliant solution was to prop me carefully supported by pillows and cushions and let me feed from a bottle without any interaction from her or anyone else. Some of this may be due to distress and some of it and some of it due to sensory overload.

Your doctor or midwife should be able to give you tips to manage the first four points. Whereas the last two are more autism specific. If the baby does not like to be held to be breastfed try altering the pressure with which you hold them. Some babies will prefer a firm hold and others a light touch. Some autistic babies will not like any touch at all which makes breast feeding very difficult. If this is the case, it does not make you or baby a failure. You could still use your breastmilk in a bottle and seat the baby so they can feed alone.

Some babies will crave touch but you as an autistic mother may not enjoy holding your baby. If this is the case it can help to understand why touch is useful for infants as they grow and develop. Ludington-Hoe (2015) states that skin-to-skin contact between a mother and their baby "promotes infant physiologic stability and warmth, helps in organizing infant sleep, reduces stress and pain (for the baby), and makes breast milk readily available." You may find that you prefer it when your baby is lying on you or when they are supported by a baby carrier close to you. You may want to experiment with holding a large weighted teddy before your baby is born.

Question:

Will there be issues for my infant around new foods/mealtimes?

Advice and Guidance:

When you are starting to introduce other foods to infants it is important to understand the sensory issues that may be present for young autistics around new foods – texture, smell and taste. In addition, there is the biological imperative to avoid eating dangerous items, which can be hard to reconcile that with young children's constant exploration of their surroundings with their mouths! In nature, bright colours often signify danger so children can be reluctant to eat brightly coloured foods.

The preference for what is known (breast milk or formula) can also impact on children's willingness to try foods that are strong tasting or smelling. As an autistic, I was one of those children who refused to eat if there was too much food in my bowl, it is better to start off with very small amounts of food so that the child can touch, smell and get used to eating foods that they can easily identify by sight/smell.

For young autistics it can be particularly helpful to be able to play with food before eating it, so that they are used to the feel of the food in their hands and mouths before swallowing. Slowly introducing new foods and textures without pressure to eat large amounts is more likely to lead to autistic children being willing and able to eat a wide variety of foods. When your child gives a clear signal that there is a particular food or texture of foods that they will not tolerate, it is better to reintroduce that food at a later date, rather than persisting right then.

Meal times should be in response to hunger if you are aiming for your child to maximise their nutritional intake. Try to use a variety of bowls/plates so that your child does not become fixated on having to have a particular plate or bowl. You can provide predictability for your child by telling them and/or using visuals to indicate upcoming meals and how they will be served. For example, saying, "Sarah, it's lunch time, we are going to eat at the table. Look Sarah, you have the blue bowl today and I have the green one. We are going to have mashed potatoes and peas." Although many autistics do not like different foods to touch, this may not apply to your child. If your child refuses to eat or gets very distressed when you put a bowl or plate of food in front of them, try having less on the plate and/or gaps between each thing in the meal. Give your child the choice of using their fingers or utensils, such as a fork, spoon or chopsticks.

Many families use high chairs for their toddlers to sit in whilst having their meals, these can be perceived by some as scary or uncomfortable and so lead to an unwillingness to sit in them and eat. If you think it may be the seating, try a variety of different eating places, such as sitting on the floor picnic style or at a low table or on your knee. Being emotionally and sensorially comfortable is vital for autistic children when they are going to be engaged in activities that are challenging for them, such as eating new foods. Bear in mind that not at all young autistics find food problematic.

Question:

At what age should by autistic daughter be ready for toilet training?

Advice and Guidance:

Every child will be ready for toilet training at a different age, and there is no optimal way to introduce this. However, with autistic girls it is very important to be very clear about what you want and why and how the child will know when they need to go to the toilet, rather than just putting them on a potty or toilet!

The basics of understanding when a girl needs to or is about to go are based in observation and biology. When the bladder fills up, it expands which makes the muscles around it stretch. Many girls will start to wiggle when they need to go, even if they are not consciously aware that they need to go to the toilet. The conscious awareness of your need to go to the toilet is part of interoception, the awareness of internal body signals. Interoception can be atypical in autistics and so it can help to specifically teach your daughter to attend to her body so that she is more able to be toilet trained.

It is important to be aware that many autistic children experience constipation which can be extremely painful, even though they are not necessarily aware of the pain. Keeping track of bowel health is very important. You can use and teach your child to use a Bristol stool chart. If your daughter does experience constipation, it is important to seek medical Advice and guidance on how to manage her bowl health. Keeping your child well hydrated and educating them about their body is important. Hydration charts show the colours of urine according to how well hydrated you are, which assists bowel health too as constipation is aggravated by dehydration. You can use visuals, cartooning and/ or spoken explanations depending on your child to explain the need to eat and drink to keep our bodies healthy, minimise headaches and constipation.

Depending on how adaptable your child is you may want to use the toilet or a potty for toilet training. Also be aware that many autistic girls struggle with bladder control for longer than their peers. They may do things like hide their wet underwear all over the house, if they are not confident that you will not be angry or disappointed with them for having toileting accidents. Bowel control and bladder control may occur at a similar age or be years apart. For children who have a lot of constipation and find passing stools (having a poo) painful, they may start to avoid this, which will make the issue worse. Increasing water and fibre intake are both helpful in this situation.

Having poo/urine charts on the toilet door will empower young children to understand and respond helpfully to their bodies needs for fluid and food, by enabling them to see how for example, drinking more water changes the colour and smell of their urine. It is better to use more factual type charts with autistic children, rather than some of the charts that replace the picture of different types of poo with food as this is confusing for literal children!

Reward charts may have no or a negative impact for autistics. It is far more useful to explain, in ways that are meaningful for your child and overly honest, about why you would like them to use the toilet and not just 'go in their underwear'. Sometimes children cannot smell or feel their toileting accidents, or they are not bothered by the smell/feeling. Unless they are explicitly told, they will not know that other people find the smell offensive. Tell your child how happy it makes you or how proud you are of them, when they use the toilet correctly. Being positive has a much more beneficial effect on the toilet training process.

Question:

How can I support my autistic daughter to develop communication?

Advice and Guidance:

Communication is the exchange of thoughts, feelings and ideas between two or more living beings. Children are thought to acquire language by being immersed in it, but it is a little more complicated for autistic children. I am a highly verbal autistic, however a few years ago I became fascinated about why some autistics were not as verbal as I was, so I asked a large number online. One of the core reasons was not knowing the reason why to communicate or not having a reason to do so.

If you always anticipate your toddler's needs by picking them up before they have time to request this in any way or giving them a drink without them needing to signal that they would like a drink, your toddler has no reason to communicate. This is because one of the most basic reasons to communicate is to express your needs and wants to that someone else so that they can meet those needs/wants. This means that you need to wait for your child to indicate needs/wants and teach them how to do so, which does not require words, but can be purely spoken words too.

Different types of communication:

All types of communication are useful when they can be understood by both/all people involved. The development of speech is supported NOT hindered by all other forms of communication.

Gestures: Gestures are body movements used to signal something. For example a wave is a gesture, often interpreted as communicating hello or goodbye. Putting both hands up towards a parent is a gesture that is used to communicate a desire to be picked up. Pointing is one of the first gestures children learn.

Sign: Sign languages are non-spoken which have both syntax and grammar. Different countries have different sign languages. Babies and children can both learn sign language, just as adults can. Learning signs will be important for the whole family if one family member is going to use signs to communicate. There are formal classes in sign as well more informal methods such as fire book lessons or YouTube.

Lo-tech visuals: Not all visuals need to be computer printed or be on an iPad or tablet. You can make your own visuals using a variety of materials, starting with paper x pens. Another simple way to make visuals is to cut pictures out of magazines or from junk mail. For example you may want to Create a really simple choice board for your child. You could cut out a picture of milk and another one of a glass of water. Then when you think your child wants a drink or after they have communicated that they want a drink, you show them both pictures and ask which one they want. You may need to teach them to look at, point to or touch the picture of the item that they want.

You can also draw your own pictures, make a simple alphabet or word board and other simple usual systems. Some older children prefer word or cartoon visuals to icons, whilst other children have a clear preference for photos or models of real objects.

High-tech visuals: There are a large number of commercial products which use a range of different technologies which suit different children. PECS – Picture exchange communication system is a product that is available in both hard copy format and as an app or software program. Prolo2go is another product that is available in these formats. Cost can be a significant factor or perkier barrier to some high tech visual communication systems, however the system may last for 10-20 years old more.

Speech: Speech is prioritized in many cultures as the "best" communication system. However, it is very important to accept that your child may not speak until much later than their peers. Some autists never speak or may only speak to a few select people. This does not mean that these autistics cannot live good, happy, fulfilling lives, especially if they do have a Communication system with which they can express their needs and wants. Many non-speaking adult autistics have taught themselves to type and in doing so have demonstrated their understanding of themselves and the world around them.

Ludington-Hoe, Susan M. "Skin-to-skin contact: a comforting place with comfort food." *MCN: The American Journal of Maternal/Child Nursing* 40.6 (2015): 359-366. Johnson, Susan L., et al. "Getting my child to eat the right amount. Mothers' considerations when deciding how much food to offer their child at a meal." Appetite 88 (2015): 24-32.

SUCCEEDING AT SCHOOL

HOW TO HELP AUTISTIC SPECTRUM GIRLS IN SCHOOL

Question:

My daughter is not toilet trained and is due to start school in a few weeks, is this a problem?

Advice and Guidance:

Yes and no. Public/state schools cannot refuse to enrol a child who is not yet toilet trained, but some schools do refuse to change diapers/nappies or can make children feel less than until they develop this skill. It is also worth bearing in mind that some children can be very cruel and toileting accidents in school, even in the first few years are rarely forgotten by classmates. If your daughter is not toilet trained yet, you can try again, explaining that most children at school use the toilet for their poos and wees and that they can be mean to children who don't. If this doesn't work if you don't feel it is appropriate for your child, then you could try buying reusable, washable incontinence underwear instead of sending them in nappies/diapers. These look like regular underwear but have built in sections that absorb liquid and are easy to wash and dry. Your daughter may well be able to self-manage these until she is toilet trained.

If, however, your daughter needs assistance to go to the toilet ensure that she has a written continence plan that all the relevant staff fully understand. Your daughter has a right to dignity and respect. If you have a choice of two schools, pick the one where this is the overwhelming attitude towards her. Never make your daughter feel bad about her developmental stage, she will make progress throughout her life, in some areas more than others, and at different rates. Kindness, compassion and respect will foster greater success than negativity and ridicule.

In addition, if your daughter still occasionally has toilet accidents just before she starts school, tell her what she needs to do if this happens, as not knowing can result in just sitting in a puddle of urine until the next break whilst getting more and more anxious about what to do. For some autistics, the smell of school toilets is so overpowering that they choose not to use them, preferring to either hold on, have accidents, or go 'elsewhere'. If this is going to be an issue for you child you can pre-empt it by asking that she have access to the accessible / disabled toilet, which is usually odour free!

Question:

What can I do to help my autistic spectrum daughter to feel like she belongs to her class at school?

Advice and Guidance:

A sense of belonging is not gained through dressing or speaking like peers, it is gained by feeling comfortable in yourself around others, where those others in turn value you and treat you with kindness. This means that your daughter is more likely to gain a sense of belonging if she has a positive attitude towards herself and does not see herself as defective or less than her peers. Teaching your daughter that all people are different, and all people have strengths and support needs can help with this positive attitude.

Question:

My daughter is highly verbal and could read and write when she started school six months ago. She doesn't see the point in school and says she wants to stay home, what should I do?

Advice and Guidance:

This is quite tricky as most children are still learning to read and write when they start school, much of the focus for the first year (or two) at school is on developing and practicing these skills, usually in a style that is unappreciated by autistics. If autistic children don't know WHY they have to attend school, they are often left bewildered about why they are dropped off by family/carers at this weird noisy place every day. On the other hand, if you have made sure they know that they go to school to learn new skills and knowledge, they can get very angry and upset if they feel that they are not learning anything new!

In addition, it is complicated by autistic girl's personality style and (usually) preference for talking to adults or much older/younger children. This results in girls not fitting in socially and in teachers and other staff assuming that they are precocious or often annoying, and these same teachers not then being aware of the gaps in social understanding and communication skills that exist for your daughter.

However, unless you wish to homeschool forever, the worst thing that you can do is to let your daughter stay home. This is because she will invariably prefer staying at home and so the school refusal will be reinforced and get worse and worse. You do have a number of options and a number of different angles to work on this from:

- Talk to your daughter about what she is learning and needs to learn at school, whether that is social or academic.

- Explain that being in some form of education is a legal requirement where you live (unless of course it is not).

- Talk to your daughter's teacher about your concerns that she is becoming frustrated and will start to exhibit challenging behaviours soon unless she becomes engaged with learning. Ask if she can do more complex reading and writing when her peers are learning to form letters or sound out three letter words.

- Explore gifted and talented programs at your daughter's school or local after school groups (being able to read and write when you start school is by default seen as gifted and talented in that area).

- Visit other schools in your area to see if they have a more flexible teaching and learning environment and if they have any vacancies. If so, visit by yourselves first and then take your daughter for a visit to see if they are a good match.

- Encourage your daughter to extend her skills at home and then take in her 'work' to show her teacher, so the teacher sees that she really can do the things you are saying she can do.

Many autistics end up changing schools frequently if there is a mismatch between their skills and needs and the teaching and learning environment provided, as when bored or frustrated our ability to moderate our behaviour becomes extremely limited, if indeed we had already developed this ability. If not, our meltdowns and shutdowns increase in intensity, frequency and sometimes duration. This behaviour in turn often results in schools assuming that these girls lack intelligence and are much less competent than is the case.

I was so excited at age three to learn to write, as I could already read and I annoyed my parents until they found a school that was willing to take me. There, I learnt to write in a big sand box, where we drew the letters with fingers or sticks, without fear of there being an imperfection left on a page should I get it wrong. When my family moved again, I must have gone to another school, but I have absolutely no memory of that school. The one after (my family moved a lot), I remember playing with students older than me and doing complex spelling, not basic spelling, which was the case for most of my five-year-old peers.

I was very lucky that most of the schools I have attended (six out of nine) assigned me work at my academic level. Of the three that did not, the first I don't recall, the second, I developed appalling behaviour and the third if I had not been leaving anyway were pressing for me to do so as my behaviour again was less than desirable. As a teacher who grew up like this, I understand that children's behaviour can be difficult for a variety of reasons, but for autistics it is usually because of one of three things; boredom, frustration or being overwhelmed (for whatever reason). However, some teachers may have no personal experience of this and not all training covers autism or other developmental differences, so you may have to share your knowledge and understanding of your daughter.

Question:

Should I disclose my daughter's autism spectrum diagnosis to her school?

Advice and Guidance:

As a teacher I say yes, please do as the more I know about your daughter, the better I can tailor my teaching to her specific needs. As a parent I say that depends on the school, will they (continue to) respect your daughter or feel that she is less than because of her diagnostic label? And finally, as an autistic advocate I say yes, but give them more information than just a label. The words autism spectrum do not convey enough information to the majority of people to be useful. You need to explain what the diagnosis means for your daughter – what are her strengths and her support needs? Preferably work with them to collaboratively develop a sensory overview (Goodall, 2018) so that they can have an in-depth understanding of who your daughter is and how to minimise her distress and anxiety whilst maximising her learning opportunities and potential to succeed in the school environment.

Question:

Should my daughter's classmates be told about her autism?

Advice and Guidance:

The school needs to know first if you would like your daughter's peers/classmates to know. The detail and specifics of what your daughter would like her peers to know about her when she is older need to be at the forefront of your mind when you are thinking about this. For example, if when she first starts school all her peers are told that she has autism and this means that she struggles to behave, those peers will hold onto that knowledge forever, and often not give her the opportunity to show that she can behave well. If on the other hand, the class learn about everyone's differences, and how there are lots of words used to describe differences, such as hair length, eye colour, wearing glasses, using a wheelchair, being autistic, speaking different languages, using a computer to communicate etc, this lays the ground for a more respectful acceptance and valuing of difference and diversity.

Even young children can sense the difference between themselves and others, but it rarely matters to them unless adults or older children signal that it should matter. I remember being on a family holiday in France when I was about eleven, my younger brother would have been three and he was happily running around the restaurant talking in English to French toddlers, who were talking back to him in French. They all played happily the entire time, no-one was in the least judgmental or concerned. The contrast between that and school children refusing to interact with peers who signed, because they "couldn't understand them" has always struck me as illogical. I am not a fluent signer, but I am happy to interact with anyone as long as they are accepting and respectful.

You need to be sure that neither your daughter, nor her peers, nor her teacher will use her autism as an excuse to say that she cannot do something, or that it makes her less than her peers in any way. She may learn some things much slower than others and she may learn some things much quicker, but she is at heart a child, in a school, to learn and grow alongside her peers in a positive and supportive environment.

You may want to discuss this issue with the principal and the teacher before making any decisions, as they may have experience around the ways to introduce differences into classroom discussion and have useful ideas. On the other hand, your daughter herself, may want to keep the information private and only share it with people she trusts and feels comfortable with. The difficulty with information is that once shared, it is impossible to take back, so you need to think forward as well as considering immediate needs.

Sharing stories about difference can be very useful with children up to age nine or ten, and these do not have to be autism specific. Elmer the Elephant is a well-known story book about the acceptance of difference and not judging too quickly. This is available as a movie/video and a book.

Question:

My grand-daughter is non-verbal, where will she go to school and how will she learn?

Advice and Guidance:

Each school district/region has their own policies about school placement, and every family has their own wishes and preferences for type of school placement. Your grand-daughter may have options of:

A special school Their local school A special class/unit attached to the local school

It is important to realise that just because your grand-daughter doesn't use speech, it does not mean she has an intellectual disability. In many school systems, access to special schools, classes and units is limited to students with an intellectual disability, usually defined as an IQ under 70. However, it is notoriously difficult to accurately assess the IQ of autistic children, in addition to which their IQ and ability to manage in school may or may not match!

When considering school placement, many families like the idea of smaller classes which usually occur in special schools, classes and units. However, other families feel that the curriculum and social offerings in these classes is too limiting for their child long term. The other factor is that education varies wildly from place to place and across time, so your experiences will not be the experiences of children today. There is no single answer to this question as it depends very much on each individual child AND the individual principals and teachers. It is rare to start school in a special setting and transfer into mainstream, but it is possible to start in mainstream and transfer to a special setting later on.

You do not need to speak to succeed educationally, what you do need however is the ability to communicate. This means that prior to school placement, if possible, your grand-daughter needs to have an assessment, usually by a speech and language therapist, to assess what communication system would be most suitable for her and the whole family. The whole family should learn to use this communication system so that your grand-daughter is truly included in the family. This does not mean that you have to stop speaking, you can continue to use speech, whilst for example signing or using picture cards to communicate.

School placement decisions may come down to which site is willing and able to communicate with your grand-daughter in ways that are meaningful to her. You can offer assistance to her parents to visit schools with them and draw up a list of questions for potential schools. Sometimes parents can struggle to do this alone as they can feel that their child is being rejected, or not valued as much as other children. If your grand-daughter has clear strengths in any area, make sure to discuss this when visiting schools too, rather than just focusing on the fact that she does not (yet) use speech to communicate.

Question:

My niece says she doesn't understand anyone else and school and that she doesn't have any friends? Is there anything I can do as she seems very lonely?

Advice and Guidance:

Yes, there are lots of things that you can do. Just listening and actually hearing her is a good start. Let her know that you believe her, as having your experiences invalidated is very demoralizing. Then there are two separate issues, both of which will be contributing to her loneliness; not understanding her peers and not having any friends. If you feel both alone and different, you start to feel deeply isolated, which can lead to loneliness and even depression. So, you and other family members need to interact with and support your niece so that she realises she is loved and supported and she can develop an understanding of her peers and she can make and sustain friends over time.

Although these are linked, they need to be addressed with different tactics. It is not possible for us autistics to learn to understand other people in one simple session or with one single explanation, however, there are some fundamentals that will help us start our life long journey of understanding other people....

Autistic children can struggle to find friends but it does not need to be impossible. One of the issues for autistic children – and adults – is that they feel different from others. Their interests tend to not be shared by their peers. Finding other children who share their interests or thinking styles can make it much easier for them to find a friend. Many autistic children have a passionate (or 'special') interest. This is likely to be shared by other children so that can be a point of similarity to build a friendship from.

While this is not always the case, autistic children often get along better with others who are neurodivergent so it can be worth introducing them to others who are autistic or have ADHD or the neurological differences.

One issue autistic children frequently experience is social anxiety. Even if there are people at school who might be friends, the sheer scale of social activity in the playground can be overwhelming for autistic children. It can be easier to meet prospective new friends in a smaller setting.

Autistic children often play differently to their neurotypical peers. They might play beside rather than with to a much older age than their typically developing peers do. It is important not to force a child to socialize in a way that you think is going to be more meaningful to them. For many autistic children, especially at younger ages playing beside a friend is preferable to playing with. Autistic children often make friends with children at a different age group. Despite understandable parental concerns of exploitation, this is usually not problematic.

Question:

Can peer mentoring help autistic girls be more comfortable in themselves and proud of who they are?

Advice and Guidance:

Peer mentoring can be very effective for autistic girls. There are some autism peer mentoring organisations such as the I CAN Network in Australia who go into schools and provide peer support and mentoring for autistic students. This is aimed at building a sense of empowerment and self-worth and to show autistic children what autistic people can achieve.

Autistic children – and girls particularly – may have low self-esteem and be very insecure around socialising. They may struggle with their sense of belonging and identity. Autistic peer mentors can provide a great example for autistic girls to aspire to. The need for belonging is often very strong in the teen years and autistic girls are no exception to this. Some girls will join peers who are negative and engaging in maladaptive behaviour, like self-harm or other risky behaviour. They may not agree with the actions of their new 'friends' but are desperate to be included and accepted. It is far better for them to relate to and look up to peers who are positively-focused. Sometimes autistic girls will try to look 'less autistic' and engage in negative behaviour to divest themselves of the 'nerd' title. However, it is preferable for them to learn to own their autistic identity through peer mentoring and be proud of who they are. This not only avoids the consequences of poor behaviour to fit in but it also gives girls a strong and positive sense of who they are which they can take with them into adult life and which can shape their self-esteem and confidence.

Being ashamed of yourself for any reason is damaging but for autistic girls, hating their autism and who they are can be toxic and impact into their adult life. Self-hatred can contribute to mental health issues and a lack of engagement in school, further education or employment. Autism is an integral part of an autistic person's character and self. It is not something you can – or would want to – 'get rid of'. So, peer mentoring in the school years to support a positive autistic identity can be incredibly beneficial. Peer mentoring can help autistic girls at different ages and circumstances.

Question:

The school wants to send my autistic grand-daughter home every time she does anything that they say is 'challenging behaviour'. I want my grand-daughter to learn how to be at school all day, how can we resolve this?

Advice and Guidance:

Often behaviour is misunderstood and misinterpreted by non-autistic people, including teachers and school staff. Perceptions around expected 'norms' can turn a harmless behaviour into one perceived as challenging. 'Challenging behaviour' can include anything from stimming to physical aggression.

In this situation it would be worth meeting with the school and spending some time in class with your daughter if possible to ascertain what the 'problem behaviour' actually is. It is important to know as much about the challenging behaviour - what it involves, if the behaviour is always or usually the same and in what situation/s it happens (time of day, in which class/es, after a similar trigger or not, in response to bullying or behaviour by other kids, after lunch or before lunch etc). Knowing this information will help you and the school address any genuinely problematic behaviour. Ask the teacher and other school staff what their concern is. It may be the case that your daughter's behaviour can be addressed through using strategies It may be the case that the behaviour is not problematic at all.

In this situation, the behaviour of the school also needs to be addressed. It does seem that the school is having difficulties providing a supportive environment for your daughter and has got to a point where they have given up trying to address the perceived difficult behaviour. By sending your daughter home every time a 'behaviour' occurs they are sending your daughter a few messages, including that if she doesn't want to stay at school all she needs to do is act in a way which will get her sent home. They are also sending the message to your daughter that she is a difficult child, a child who does not fit in the school environment and presumably beyond that, society, that her autism – and she – is problematic. None of these are messages you want your daughter receiving from school. Changing the school's behaviour may in fact be harder than changing your daughter's behaviour! Ideally you and the school need to work through the issues in a collegiate way, with your daughter's needs at the center.

Understanding 'challenging behaviors'

In some cases 'challenging behaviors' are in response to aggression, bullying or teasing from others, or from extreme anxiety or your child feeling threatened and confused by activities at school.

Autistic children's behaviour can come from root causes that you or the school may not be aware of. They may be highly anxious about different elements of school life, from relationships with peers to issues around food and toilet facilities. They may not understand why they are at school at all. Things like them being too hot or too cold or being in pain but not having the interoceptive awareness to know this is happening can have a huge impact on behaviour. They may be dehydrated, hot, cold or constipated. This might sound simple to address but many children can be in significant physical distress but not be consciously aware of it. Doing some work around in-

teroception can benefit children exhibiting challenging behaviours.

One of the key factors in challenging behaviour for autistic children is atypical interoception. Interoception
is your sense of your internal self; your temperature,
muscle state, breathing rate, thirst etc. Without accurate interoception, it is not possible to tell when our
emotional state is changing, and for some autistics,
they are not able to recognize how they feel (alexithymia). When we experience negative emotions, our
sympathetic nervous system is usually activated. If
we know this, by for example realizing we are getting
angry, we can do something about it.

If due to poor interoception, we do not know we
are getting angry, the anger builds and builds until our sympathetic nervous system is overloaded. At
this point the human survival instinct kicks in and
we literally lose the ability to think, instead moving into fight, flight or freeze (flop/drop) behaviour.
Most people have a default of one of these, but when
stressed further, by for example being approached,
escalate the survival instinct into fight. Both flight
and fight are regularly misinterpreted as challenging behaviour. Teaching your child or grandchild interoceptive awareness by for example both doing the
activities in Interoception 101 from South Australia
(Goodall, 2016).

Question:

We just got our daughter's first school report and
it said that 'like many autistic children, Jess has
splinter skills in maths. What does this mean?

Advice and Guidance:

The idea of 'splinter skills' relates to the concept autistic children and adults being proficient in one or more areas whilst having challenges in another. Some autistic children are told they are 'twice exceptional' as well. This usually relates to having 'gifts' in one area but having difficulties coping in others.

It is important to be aware that having giftedness or splinter skills does not mean your child needs any less support. Children with twice exceptional and splinter skills can really struggle due to their difficulties being overlooked because of their high performance in one or other area. In some instances, those twice exceptional skills are seen as 'so what' skills due to the difficulties the child experiences in other areas of life.

An example of 'so what' skills is the ability to name every car by make and model on sight or the ability to play computer games to a very high level. However, those skills can be a source of self-worth and pride. The authors of this book both have some 'gifts,' one of which is the capacity to write this book. With splinter skills and twice exceptional skills it is important to be clear that the skills alone don't mean much more than what they are. Someone being highly proficient at one thing doesn't necessarily translate into skills in other parts of life. Autistic children with 'splinter skills' need to be supported just as mic as those without such skills.

Question:

My autistic daughter refuses to do many of the activities in school, her teachers are getting very frustrated with her and say we are spoiling her when we don't make her do the missed work at home. Should we make her do the work or should we be finding a new school for her?

Advice and Guidance:

There is no straightforward answer to this as it very much depends on why your daughter is not doing her school work. There are a couple of 'typical' reasons why autistic children and young people do not join in with school activities; boredom, frustration, sensory or emotional overload, anxiety, depression, fear of failure (perfectionism), fear of peers or teacher (due to bullying), being in pain (whether or not they can communicate that) or being distracted and not hearing or processing the instructions are the most common. Without knowing why your daughter is not doing activities you can't pick an effective strategy to improve things.

Asking your daughter is a good start, but if she is too young or not able to communicate in a way that gives you the information you need, observation in class is the next starting point. If she is bored because the work is too easy or meaningless, teaching her through her passions or interests is an easy way to increase her engagement in learning. If you or the school notice that she seems withdrawn or completely inactive, this may be a shutdown, which is the freeze part of the human survival instinct, resulting from sympathetic nervous system overload. Teaching interoception activities in school and/or getting your daughter to do interoception activities with you before arriving at school can help her to not become overloaded during the day as well as helping her learn her body's signals so that she can respond earlier and prevent meltdowns/shutdowns.

However, it is really important to ensure that your daughter is actually aware of what they are meant to be doing. If you have never had an auditory processing assessment, it would be worth finding out if she can process multi-step instructions or only three, two or single step instructions. This is vital information for a school to have so they can tailor the communication to your daughter to maximize her educational success.

Question:

My daughter refuses to wear her school uniform as she says that it is itchy.

Advice and Guidance:

Under disability discrimination laws in most countries, organizations, including schools need to make reasonable accommodations for people with disabilities. The sensory sensitivities of children and young people on the spectrum are not always taken very seriously, but to the person experiencing them, they are as real as your sensory experience is to you. It should be possible for you to negotiate a different fabric in the same colour for your daughter. Another issue that regularly comes up in this context it shoes. In some areas, such as New Zealand, many primary/elementary school children do not wear shoes in class, instead leaving them at the door. In other countries, shoes are expected to be worn at school in the classroom. This is problematic for some autistics who intensely dislike wearing shoes. You could negotiate for a reasonable accommodation of different footwear.

PUBERTY

Puberty is a difficult time for most young people but for autistic girls it can be particularly challenging. Physical and emotional puberty can come at different times for autistic young people meaning that their bodies are maturing but their interests may not reflect the changes to their bodies. Their peers may be become interested in boyfriends and girlfriends and looking at and being sexually attracted to people from popular culture such as musicians and actors, whilst autistic girls experiencing puberty may have little or no interest in those things and spend their time playing Minecraft or My Little Pony or other less traditionally mature pursuits. And along with emotional and maturity challenges, the significant physical changes which occur in puberty can be very difficult and distressing to experience. Pubic hair, periods, growing breasts and changing body shape and hormones and all that go with that can be very distressing for autistic girls.

Question:

I am dreading my daughter's first period because she has so many sensory issues. How can I prepare her for puberty?

Advice and Guidance:

In this situation, it is often the case that knowledge equals power. Discuss the changes which are likely to happen and what your daughter will need to do when she reaches puberty. You can preempt some sensory issues by discussing them with your daughter and working out in consultation with her some of the strategies that she can use. You can also make a social story or similar on puberty changes which your daughter can refer to when she needs to. The best thing in this situation is preparation.

Be available to your daughter if she has questions and try to establish a relationship based in teamwork with your daughter as much as you can. Puberty is a challenge that you can work on and address together. Be sure to explain that although she may find the smell of her blood overpowering that it is highly unlikely that other people can ever smell it. Many girls worry about other people smelling their blood and find this as or more upsetting than the actual smell itself.

Question:

Are sanitary towels/pads better for autistic girls than tampons?

Advice and Guidance:

Some autistic women and girls do not like the feeling of penetration by anything, including a tampon. Some autistic girls and women find tampons difficult to insert correctly which leads to discomfort. Some autistic girls and women may forget if a tampon is inserted and for how long. Some girls can be quite anxious about tampons as there are warnings on the packets about a rare condition called toxic shock syndrome which can happen in a tiny minority of instances of using tampons, but this small possibility can cause anxiety. For these people sanitary pads are probably a better choice.

However, some autistic girls and women prefer to use tampons, finding sanitary pads uncomfortable or unable to satisfactorily contain the smell of their blood. Tampons can have a number of advantages over sanitary pads: You can swim or play sport while wearing them, there is less of an issue with odour and if they are inserted correctly you can almost not be aware they are there. Really it is up to the individual girl or young woman. There may need to be a time of experimentation with different products to see which works best for your daughter.

There are also other options available these days that may not have been available in years gone by; menstrual cups, period proof underwear and hormone controlling options. Menstrual cups are also inserted into the vagina and they collect the blood which is then washed off when the cup is removed. Cups can be left in place for up to 12 hours and are made of medical grade silicon usually. Odor is very low when they are in use.

Period proof underwear is designed to look like regular underwear but acts like a sanitary pad, collecting all the blood which is then washed out when the underwear is washed. For light to moderate flows, this is probably a very good, though initially expensive option, for girls and women who struggle to manage with other options and do not want to go with hormone controlling options.

It is important to teach and encourage good hygiene around all sanitary products, such as washing hands before and after using a product. In addition, girls and women need to know when is it time to change a pad or tampon, cup or underwear and what do you do with used sanitary products? Reusable items such as cups or period proof underwear often need to be sterilized or washed, in particular ways, before reuse and it is important that instructions provided on purchase are followed.

Question:

I have read about the double puberty experienced by autistics, what is this and what does it mean for my daughter?

Advice and Guidance:

Biological puberty is due to hormones/physical changes and emotional/psychological puberty is due to a growing awareness and interest in sexuality and relationships. For many people the two occur at the same sort of time and are often thought of as one thing. However, for many autistics, the two puberties do not occur at the same time with hormonal changes occurring months or even years before the young person starts to be interested in sex and/or relationships. It is unknown why this is the case, but it can cause social issues as autistic girls are physically developmentally the same as their peers but emotionally and psycho-socially much younger. If this is the case for your daughter it is important to ensure she has access to safe social events and activities where she can continue to be herself, without being socially ostracized.

Question:

Sarah used to have lots of friends in primary school, but in the last year as her friends have started dating and being very interested in teenage things, she seems to have been left behind. Does this happen a lot?

Advice and Guidance:

This is a common experience for autistic teens and young women. Emotional puberty and maturity can happen quite a long time after physical puberty for autistic girls. However, their neurotypical peers tend to reach emotional and physical puberty at around the same time. This can result in autistic girls feeling and/or being left out socially as their interests are more likely to remain similar to those they had in primary school while their peers are looking for relationships and sexual experiences. One way to address this is to ensure autistic girls have contact - and hopefully make friends with - other autistic girls who may be in a similar situation and so might share similar interests and games. It is important to be aware that some autistic teens do start engaging in sexual activity quite young, either out of choice, because they find it enjoyable, or through coercion. Again, the more knowledge a girl has the more empowered she will be to avoid exploitation and make positive choices about her developing sexuality.

Autistic young women may seem naive and childish to their neurotypical peers and this can be used as an excuse for bullying. When autistic young women mature sexually they may have no role modelling around how to manage this, which can lead to issues being singled out by predators. It is very important to teach young autistic people and perhaps particularly young women, some boundaries and self-protection skills where they can identify if someone is behaving inappropriately. Below is a table showing some signs of inappropriate / predatory behaviour and some safety strategies.

It is important to note that while by far the most common sexual abuse and threatening behaviour is done by men against women, this is not the only kind of abuse and threat and women can prey upon other women in some cases. Just because the person doing the inappropriate behaviour is female does not mean it isn't abusive or threatening. The perpetrators of sexual violence are not all neurotypical. Some autistic people can prey upon others too so just because a person is on the spectrum does not necessarily mean they are a safe person.

Teaching autistic teens and adults about the difference between safe, positive, healthy relationships and unhealthy, unsafe, negative relationships is very important. As many autistics are gender non-conforming and/or not heterosexual, it is important to provide as much information about as many types of relationships as needed. A good resource for this is: The Autism Spectrum Guide to Sexuality and Relationships: Understand Yourself and Make Choices that are Right for You, by Dr Emma Goodall (2016).

Safety strategies for young women on the autism spectrum
Always ensure parents/carers know where the young woman is going to be and ensure she checks in with parents frequently by message or phone.
Ensure a young woman has trustworthy company when she goes out.

Safety strategies for young women on the autism spectrum
Ensure young woman understands the concepts of: ▶ Consent and what it means in practical situations ▶ That her body is hers and she is the only one who decides what to do with it ▶ The warning signs for abuse and threatening behaviour above
Teach physical self-defence and explain the situations in which it is OK to use it.
Build self-esteem and self-confidence.
Encourage the young woman to walk with an upright, confident posture and not to make eye contact with anyone when out alone.
Ensure the young woman has a phone with enough credit to call parents or trusted adults when out and ensure that they know emergency numbers and when to use them.

Safety strategies for young women on the autism spectrum

Teach autistic young women that it is OK to say no to requests for sex whatever the other person says, for example if they tell a story about how they are sad and depressed, but sex will make them happier, or that they should do things to show that they love the person.

Talk about safety regularly and encourage the young woman to talk through any concerns she has.

Make sure the young woman is aware that almost all abusers are known to their victims so focusing on 'stranger danger' is not much use in itself.

Problematic behaviour

Giving the young women drugs or alcohol with the intent to make them intoxicated. If somebody keeps buying you drinks or drugs, this can be a warning sign that they are attempting to make you intoxicated to make you less inhibited, usually to have sex with you.

Following you home without asking or overstepping boundaries. An example is if you say you don't want them to come home with you and they ignore your wishes.

Problematic behaviour
Continuing behaviour which makes you uncomfortable and/or continuing this behaviour when you ask or tell them to stop.
Somebody repeatedly buying you gifts can be a sign that they wish to 'bribe' you for sexual acts.
Stalking behaviour and online behaviour which makes you feel uncomfortable or threatened or which people you trust tell you seems to be predatory or creepy.
Sending or requesting explicit images or words (images of genitalia, 'dirty talk') online.
Telling you to keep things secret - 'Don't tell your mum about this. It is our secret...'
Tricking you into do something you do not wish to do, especially sexual acts. 'Everyone else is doing this. We should do it too. It will make you really popular. If you loved me you would do this.'
Posting sexual images of you online without your consent and other posting images which you consider shameful or embarrassing.

Question:

I am an autistic mum and I am extremely empathic and now my kids are teenagers it is just awful in our house as their teenage melodrama is really distressing for me and then I start to yell and scream and then this makes my youngest have a meltdown. How can we manage things better?

Advice and Guidance:

Scheduling your own space - both in terms of physical space and also human contact - can help address this issue although the problem is likely to continue for some time, so you might have to try a few different physical setups and messaging to your kids to ensure you and they get adequate quiet, alone time.

It is important to try to avoid blaming your children for your overload when you speak with them as this can be incredibly difficult for them to hear and can damage your relationships into the long-term. It is a good idea when you and your kids are calm, to talk through the issues and work out strategies which might work for both you and them.

If both you and your kids can learn to identify signs that things are escalating towards meltdown - yours or theirs - that can make it easier to deescalate before a full meltdown occurs. If you cannot, it would be useful for you to develop your interoception by learning how to notice your internal body signals.

You do need to acknowledge though that this is a difficult situation and there will almost certainly be times when things get out of control. It is not a matter of placing blame but more one of learning from it and reminding yourself this is a stage you're and your children may need to go through, but which is likely to resolve as your children grow older and more mature and probably move out of home. This situation is often an ongoing journey. It involves setting and respecting boundaries, communicating with your kids about your and their expectations and learning from setbacks. It is difficult but not insurmountable. It can be really helpful to see it as a project for all of you to work on together rather than 'mum against the kids'.

For some parents, it is important to have quiet time before bed each night, whereas for others it is more important to have a family routine. Only with time will you work out what you need to make sure you have the energy to manage parenting your teen(s). All parents find parenting difficult at times, it is ok to find this difficult and very important to take care of your needs, otherwise you cannot take care of your children's needs.

You might decide to use some strategies that are often considered for children at school, such as headphones or schedules. Whatever works for you and your family. If you have a two or more-adult household, you could also each provide sometime within the week that is solely for each adult as quiet time, either in or out of the house.

Question:

My daughter has one friend, a girl from her class at school. I think that they are having a relationship. What should I do about it?

Advice and Guidance:

In the same way as if your daughter has a relationship with a young man, the key concerns here are as to whether your daughter is being respected by her girlfriend and that the relationship is not exploitative, abusive or damaging to your daughter.

Many autistic people are non-heterosexual. Some are asexual, but many have an interest in forming relationships or having sexual encounters with other people, whatever their gender. For parents who, for whatever reason, have issues accepting those who are lesbian, gay, bisexual, pansexual or have another non-heterosexual sexuality, it is very important to put this thinking on hold.

Whatever your thoughts about lesbian relationships might be your daughter needs your love and support. People who have non-heterosexual sexualities face significantly increased rates of bullying and if that person is autistic as well then this may reach a crisis point that can tip your daughter into depression or suicidal ideation. If they know their parent/s support them in having a girlfriend then this can be a very important part of supporting them and preventing them from developing suicidal ideation.

This is not just about being nice or 'politically correct'. Suicide rates among autistic young people and those who are lesbian, gay, bisexual, transgender, intersex, Queer and questioning are significantly higher. The difference between their parent/s being supportive or not could be a critical factor in building self-acceptance and love. If you think your daughter is having a relationship with another young woman, then there is no need to put her on the spot and ask about the nature of her relationship. What you can do is create an environment where she knows that it is OK with her family if she is in a lesbian relationship. You could do this by watching movies with positive lesbian characters or by mentioning some well-known lesbian women in conversation and saying positive things about them.

Be aware of the messages you send. Some autistic young people will read in a lot more information than is intended, particularly when it comes to a topic which is sensitive for them such as their sexuality.

In countries where same sex marriage is legal, it may be easier for young women to be more confident and public about their sexuality.Basically, creating an environment where 'gay is OK' is going to be of benefit whether your daughter is in a relationship with her friend or not. How you approach your daughter's partner - if she is their partner - will be similar to how you as a parent would manage your daughter's relationship with a young man. Use your judgement as to whether or not to intervene if you are aware that there are issues which are likely to result in your daughter being abused, taken advantage of or humiliated by her partner, be available for your daughter to talk to about the relationship if she wants and be as aware as you can about the partner in case anything potentially damaging happens.

Question:

My (male) child has been telling me for a few years that they are really a girl. Now that puberty has arrived, they are getting more and more distressed by not being seen by the rest of the world as female. With their autism they are really blunt and many family members have stopped talking to us, saying that we need to tell our child what is what and stop pandering to their silly ideas. What should I be doing? Is it possible for an autistic to be transgender or transsexual?

Advice and Guidance:

It seems your child may be transgender. Gender dysphoria is where a person's physical (and present from birth) sex characteristics differ from their identity resulting in their wanting/needing to transition to a different gender in order to be truly themselves. It is relatively common amongst autistic people and there are a large number of transgender autistic people, including teens and young people. It has been suggested that as many as 25 percent of autistic people are gender divergent. Some autistic people are gender fluid, meaning they do not identify with having a fixed gender and non-binary gender - meaning they do not identify as male or female but either something in and between or fluid.

If a young person has expressed for some time that they feel they do not identify with the gender they were born as then it is highly likely they are transgender, gender fluid or gender non-binary. This is not a bad thing. In actuality, when a trans person has their gender identity respected and validated it is usually a very positive thing helping them to feel genuinely happy in themselves, often for the first time ever. A parent supporting their trans child or young person is a huge protective factor for their development to be a well-adjusted adult who values and respects themselves.

Unfortunately, there are some highly unhelpful attitudes about gender diversity. Some people feel very threatened by differences and some are just plain bigoted. It makes life for trans and non-binary people a lot harder than it needs to be and this is particularly the case for children and young people. It is very sad if some of your family members no longer speak with you. However, this says a lot more about them than it does about you or your child.

A good course of action for you and your child to take is to do some research about gender identity and gender dysphoria. If you child wants to take steps towards transitioning, you will need to see a doctor who specializes in gender dysphoria. There is quite an exhaustive process involved in transitioning. It is not just a simple process where you go to the chemist and get some male or female hormones! If you or your child knows others who have transitioned or are transitioning it can be great to share thoughts and experiences. Some transgender kids and their parents who seek medical advice early can be given drugs which block puberty. This can make life a lot easier for someone who is transitioning.

The most important thing you can do as a parent is to love and support your child and validate their journey whatever it may be.

Question:

I am worried that one of the autistic girls that I teach is being taken advantage of by some of the other students. I think they are getting her to sell drugs for them and using her for sex. How do I talk to her or her family about this to find out what is really going on?

Advice and Guidance:

It is sadly quite common for autistic girls and young women to be taken advantage of by predators, whether their peers or older people. Raising this either with the girl or her family is likely to be a very difficult conversation. If what you suspect is indeed the case, the girl may not be aware that what is happening is harmful or unusual. She may have been given an idea of 'friendship' in exchange for sexual favours and selling drugs. For autistic people who are isolated, lonely and excluded the very idea of having friends and belonging socially may be highly prized. This means that some autistics may be willing to do unpleasant and illegal things, to have that sense of social acceptance.

Whatever the reason, selling drugs is a crime, so this is a really sensitive area. While judges will usually take mitigating circumstances into consideration, like someone being taken advantage of, not every judge will. This means that if the girl is charged with drug trafficking she may face the same level of legal sanctions as someone who was 'genuinely' involved in drug trafficking.

In relation to sexual assault and abuse, if you think this is happening there may be a duty of care for you to report this to police or child protection authorities as part of your role as a teacher. In this case, it is recommended NOT to talk through things with the girl because it may put a barrier in place to prosecuting the offenders. If you speak with the girl, it is important to consider the following:

- She may not realize she is being taken advantage of
- She is likely to have very low self-esteem and not have a strong identity and little sense of who she is
- She may identify with the people abusing her
- She may not want to lose her 'friends'
- She may be very frightened and unhappy, but she may not realize this
- She may have alexithymia (emotion blindness) or very poor interoception (awareness of self) so not actually know how she feels about the situation
- She might be afraid to speak with you about this as it is 'wrong'. This means that establishing a trusting relationship where she can confide in you is important.
- When talking to the girl's parents it is important to consider the following:
- They may be in denial that there is a problem
- They may respond to you or their daughter with anger rather than understanding
- There may be issues around the girl's autism diagnosis - family members may not recognize it or

currently misunderstand autism in an unhelpful, unsupportive way

▸ Family members may blame the girl for her actions and not realize it is due to her being taken advantage of

▸ Family members might want to take actions – such as physically attacking the drug dealers, which while understandable is very likely to do more harm than good

▸ Family members may respond with horror and sorrow about what is happening and blame themselves

It may be that your concerns about the girl are unfounded and she is not being taken advantage of. For this reason, you may need to think about how to present the issue to the girl or her parents. If there is strong evidence, then it might be a good idea to approach the conversation from the starting point of 'I think there might be something damaging going on...'and keeping it clear throughout the conversation this is something which actually might not in fact not be occurring. However, if you are reasonably certain, it is better to let the police and/or child protection authorities investigate and find out the full story.

Goodall, E. (2018) Understanding and Facilitating the Achievement of Autistic Potential. SA: Healthy Possibilities.

WHERE TO NEXT

HELPING AUTISTIC SPECTRUM GIRLS CHOOSE POST SCHOOL OPTIONS

Question:

What are the options for autistic spectrum girls leaving school?

Advice and Guidance:

Autistic girls potentially have all the same options available to them on leaving school as other people do, although there can be some difficulties to overcome to ensure post-school options work well. The sorts of opportunities available for people leaving school include university, polytechnic or college courses - either degree courses or individual accredited subjects offered through online providers. There are also options in vocational training / trade school / apprenticeships or moving straight into work after school.

None of these options is intrinsically better or worse than another. Instead each option suits a different individual. As much as possible, the choice of post-school option should be driven by the person undertaking it themselves, in consultation with their parent/s or carers and other trusted adults. It is rarely wise to make a decision on behalf of somebody else in terms of their study or career path. Even if you think your daughter may become an excellent chef or electrical engineer, unless she wants to try it, it is unlikely to be successful if you make her follow a given pathway.

The different kinds of options for school leavers depend on what level of schooling the girl has completed, practical issues (such as the location of further education campus and transport and housing options and costs and accessibility) and of course their own wishes and interests. It can be advisable to start the conversation on what post-school options your daughter would like to undertake quite early. Moving from school to further education or work is a significant change for all young people but for autistic young women it can be particularly challenging due to anxiety around things that are unknown or very different. You can discuss things around what they would like to do after school and work through whether it is feasible and answer any questions to address concerns or anxiety around taking this new step. As with any change, the level of support required by an autistic person can increase when taking on a new challenge like work or further education. In addition to family and peer support, assistance is available at many education institutions in the form of disability student services, or at work through disability employment services. Work experience or volunteering opportunities in a range of areas can be very useful to enable people to gain a real-life insight into the actuality of a range of jobs and careers.

Open days at colleges/universities or polytechnics can provide excellent opportunities to visit campuses and look at the practical aspects of location, transport and potential sensory or other issues as well as to meet staff members. Some further education campuses have accommodation on site or close by and if this is something you or your daughter are considering, it is a good idea to do a visit prior to applying and to ensure the accommodation is suitable. This visit will also be a good starting point to open the discussion about hidden curriculum rules involved in shared houses or other types of student accommodation.

Question:

Are some careers more suited to autistic spectrum girls than others?

Advice and Guidance:

A lot of conventional thinking suggests that autistic people will be better or worse at particular jobs, depending on factors like the level of customer contact, relative stress of the work itself, level of responsibility, busyness of the work environment and other factors. In many cases it is true that autistic women prefer to work in a quieter environment with minimal or no customer contact, but this is not applicable to all autistic women. There are autistic women working successfully in all sorts of industries including such apparently autism unfriendly fields as real estate, beauty therapy, lawyers of various specialties, children's party performers and high school teachers - all careers which traditionally would not be considered 'autism friendly'.

It is often the case that the type of job is less relevant than the environment of the workplace or the interest level of the person in the job. For example, sensory overload experienced anywhere is going to be distressing for an autistic employee. Even if they were working in the most traditionally autism friendly job, they would struggle to function if the sensory issues were not addressed. Therefore, having a supportive manager who recognizes the need to address sensory and communication issues is probably going to be more important than the nature of the work itself. If a workplace has staff who are welcoming and respectful, that may make a huge difference to the autistic woman's sense of wellbeing and engagement at work.

If an autistic woman is able to work in an area of interest or passion, then she is likely to be more comfortable, less stressed and more successful. Many autistics enjoy self-employment in obscure areas of interest, such as insects. Other autistics have joined family businesses or gained work through volunteer placements. However, some autistics are able to gain and retain work in a range of fields both with and without tertiary qualifications.

While a response to this question could be that autistic women prefer to be librarians or academics and that is what they should aim for, in fact that is not a helpful statement. A suitable career will be the career that a woman chooses and finds works for her. There is a difficulty around saying one or other industry or career is somehow better than another. The best career is one which is interesting and engaging and where the employee feels supported and comfortable. In terms of finding a good career for your autistic daughter - or yourself - the key is often their interests and preferences, not some arbitrary notion of this or that job won't work for autistic people. If your career is driven by your interests, you feel accepted and supported by managers and colleagues and you can build and grow your skills, that is a good career.

It is also worth noting that careers can change over the course of a person's working life so not many people will just do one kind of work for the rest of their life. Additionally, speech is not a requirement for some jobs and that autistics without speech have both enjoyed and been successful at work. Some organizations specialize in trying to match real job opportunities with autistic applicants, whilst other organizations provide supported accommodation opportunities.

Question:

What if my autistic daughter can never work? How can she have a good life after school?

Advice and Guidance:

In our society we have a number of unhelpful, loaded terms and thoughts which go with employment and unemployment. The question 'what do you do?' aimed at an adult is one of these loaded terms. The subtext to that question is 'What do you do for work?' and beyond that unsaid questions stemming from it like 'Do you earn a lot of money?' But when a person has to answer that question and they do not work, it is a horrible thing because with that question comes an assumption of social value around employment. If someone doesn't work they are often seen as or can feel devalued with a range of unhelpful assumptions and judgment about their unemployment.

Work is a great thing and most human beings find it engaging and would struggle if they no longer had the focus of tasks and socialising which work involves, let alone the more tangible effects of working such as income. Not working is on the list of things which are considered as 'losing' in the race of life. This kind of thinking is exclusionary and not helpful for anyone. However, being involved in meaningful activities, whether paid or not, can be of great benefit to someone's well being and mental health.

Some autistic people can only work a few hours, cannot work at all or have become so demoralized by looking for jobs and getting knocked back that they have given up looking. This is not their fault, and neither is it a measure of their lack of value or worth.

If you or your daughter cannot work that should not be a reason for judgement. We need to move beyond the notion that the only value a person can have is if they work. Another issue around not working if you are autistic is the pity and paternalism which that can entail as well as the idea that a person is 'not contributing' through not working. These are terrible things for a young person or her parent/s or carers to deal with.

The counter to this view is to question the value of social 'worth.'

Answering the question of how somebody who doesn't work can have a good and fulfilled life after school essentially comes down to interest and engagement. The will to work, or be engaged in meaningful activity, is a strong one, so even people who don't do paid work tend to engage in some kind of activity, albeit unpaid. Autistic people tend to have at least one consuming passion. For an autistic person pursuing their passion is usually incredibly rewarding. Challenging the view that a 'special' interest is an unhelpful obsession - unless the interest is negative, damaging or dangerous - it is useful to encourage the young woman to pursue her interest. For some autistic people this has led to careers as writers or artists, scientists and entrepreneurs, to name a few.

Even if the outcome is that the young woman doesn't create a career through their interest, it is almost certainly going to be fulfilling for her to engage in her interest anyway. When speaking about activity and employment, fulfilment can be the main goal.

While some autistic people need little or no social contact, connecting with others is very important for other autistics. Autistic friendships may look different to these of our non-autistic peers and colleagues but a fulfilled life for most autistic people will involve social contact with people and often with animals as well.

It is important to ensure as much as possible that a person who does not work is fulfilled and able to engage socially if they wish to. For many autistic women this can happen through social media and online communication. Many women find lasting friendships online - the two authors of this book met online, and this is their fourth book together!

Question:

How can autistic spectrum girls be helped to choose a post school pathway that will enable them to live good lives?

Advice and Guidance:

The concept of a 'good life' varies with each individual. It is best not to focus too much on specifics around fulfilment. For example, it would be better to want your daughter to be doing something which challenges her, but she enjoys, than to pick out a particular course or job which you like but she may not be interested in. Some young people will follow a career path set by a parent in order to please their parents or because they do not understand there are other options. However, following a career is something which requires strong motivation. If your daughter is not motivated to do that job or course of study but doing it because you want her to, it will be much harder for her to engage in it and may have unintended consequences such as disengaging from work or study.

One of the key roles of a parent is to guide their child through school age education to further study and then work. With autistic girls this can be the case, but is not always. Some people will not have the capacity for employment or further education for a variety of reasons. It is important not to be disheartened by this. As discussed above, a person's worth is not limited by their career or their salary or what kind of car they drive. The concept of a 'post school pathway' might conjure images of a clear trajectory going from school to university to professional job. For many on the autism spectrum as well as neurotypical young people, this idea of a trajectory is in fact unhelpful. For many autistic young people, their pathway is more closely related to a winding journey than a straight path. This does not need to be a negative thing.

For parents, trying to support your child to choose a pathway when in fact they are exploring different parts of the education and career journey can backfire and result in the opposite outcome – a young woman who becomes disengaged and resentful and who might struggle to reengage with work or study. While parents giving guidance and support is often very helpful for a young person they often make the best choices through an approach which looks more like facilitation than management. For example, if your daughter wants to study visual art but you are concerned there is no money in such a path, flatly telling her that she can't study visual art tends to be a lot less helpful than working through her study and career options in the visual art field – research available careers in that area, look at qualifications preferred or required for such jobs etc.

Put simply, supporting your daughter to build her understanding of what post school options she is interested in and to empower her and support her on the path she chooses is a great start. Giving her support but also setting boundaries and helping her to acquire useful skills for post school study and / or work is very helpful. Some of these skills are:

▸ Responsibility
▸ Time management

- Resilience
- Confidence
- The ability to think independently
- The ability to ask for help
- Awareness of safe and unsafe people
- Strategies to address anxiety and / or perfectionism
- Self worth

Many of these qualities are not things your daughter will be able to acquire quickly and form part of her ongoing learning.

Question:

How can I teach my autistic daughter to self-advocate to ensure barriers to her success at college or university or work can be broken down?

Advice and Guidance:

Self-advocacy usually comes from a place of self-worth, pride and acceptance. A young woman who struggles to accept or discuss her autism is likely to struggle significantly if she is expected to advocate for herself. Most people are not at either end of the self-esteem and self-acceptance 'spectrum' though. Most of us – including autistic young people – sit somewhere between the poles of disliking ourselves and feeling that our autism is negative and at the other end, being proud of who we are and wanting to change the world through sharing our experiences of autism. Young people are often less proud or accepting of themselves, but this is not always the case. In order to put a young woman in the position of being able and willing to advocate for herself, building up her confidence and self-worth is an important place to start.

Self-advocacy takes a few different forms. In further education, self-advocacy is useful to ensure the student gets what she needs and is supported to learn in the way that she learns. This requires a practical sort of advocacy involving possibly speaking with lecturers and disability student services about how she can best be supported. Advocacy often, but not always, gets respected and results in a positive response – for example your daughter getting the right support from disability student services to complete her subjects in an inclusive and supportive way.

Another kind of advocacy is where there is an injustice – ableism, prejudice, bullying and so forth. This kind of advocacy is often harder and may require more than just the student herself advocating. As parents it might seem the obvious step to go in 'all guns blazing' to fix the issue but this can be counterproductive. It might be a better course of action to discuss the issue with your daughter and see what supports she needs – and wants – and go about accessing that. Most young adults – autistic or not – would not welcome their mum or dad coming into a lecture and telling off the academic as they stood at the lectern!

One of the best things to promote the ability and capacity for self-advocacy is to ensure your daughter is in contact with other autistic people and preferably some experienced self-advocates. Autistic adults can be great role models for autistic young people and friends of a similar age can share their own experiences of further education and advocating for themselves. The autistic peer group is filled with advocates of all ages, and most of them do not have an 'autism advocate' on their CV and may not even realize they are doing advocacy.

If your daughter advocates for herself in further education, it sets a precedent and works to break down barriers not just for her but for others that come after her. On the next page is a checklist of some issues and challenges which can arise in further education along with some possible strategies or solutions.

Independent learning

The transition from school to further education is a big change for a variety of reasons. One issue which autistic young people often struggle with is moving from the more supported learning model at school to more independent study in further education settings. One of the strategies around addressing this is for parent/s to provide information on how the level of support may differ to their daughter well in advance of her starting post-school study.

You can start to build your daughter's ability to study in a more independent setting through practice and preparation. You can set exercises around transitioning to the new environment while your daughter is at school and can talk to her about what further education is like in terms of the need for motivation and focus, then work through any concerns she has prior to starting post-school study.

Change

Change is something most autistic people, and many neurotypical people too, find challenging. The change from school to further education is a significant one. Autistic young people know school. Even if they don't particularly enjoy it, it is at least a reasonably predictable and known space. Further education is not.

Autistic people often benefit from having a 'road map' or mental picture of a new situation, not just the physical, built environment but also what sorts of things the change will involve; what kinds of people will be in the new setting, what sorts of things they will be expected to do and how will the day be divided.

Getting your daughter used to the campus and what transport she will need to get to class is probably the easy bit. Concerns around how days will be structured, what kinds of things she will be doing, and the different job roles of academic staff may be harder to prepare her for. It may help for you to contact the administration area at the university or other education provider your daughter is going to and explain your daughter is autistic, providing she has consented to you sharing this, and asking them to provide as much information as they can to assist your daughter in transiting to further study.

Social interactions

Starting study in a new place filled with unknown people, students as well as academic staff, is very challenging for most autistic people. Memories of being excluded and / or bullied at school may linger and cause significant anxiety around meeting new student colleagues. Being in a new place AND meeting new people who they will be spending time with is often very anxiety-provoking and can be overwhelming.

You can talk to your daughter about how people in further study have chosen to be there and probably value academic learning, unlike in school where many of the children, and probably the bullies, were only there because they had to be. Although there are a few exceptions to this, this means that generally university students all share a wish to succeed and an interest in academic study and so are likely to be more understanding and supportive (although noting there can be unhelpful competition between students resulting in poor behaviour).

Your daughter in further education is an adult, with all that entails. At university and other education providers, there can be a number of 'adult'-type things going on, like drinking alcohol, engaging in sexual activity and relationships. There is no reason why autistic adults shouldn't drink alcohol in moderation or engage in consensual sexual activity but your daughter needs to be aware of these things and to understand her rights and responsibilities. This may be an ongoing conversation, but it is essential to ensure she has an understanding of these things to help avoid some of the difficulties which can arise.

Time management

Independent learning requires skills around time management and prioritising, Some autistic people have executive functioning difficulties which impact these skills. This can mean that despite having an incredible understanding of the subject matter your daughter may turn up to the exam on the wrong day or not at all. This is most often not 'vagueness' or a lack of discipline but an issue of how the brain is wired. No amount of discipline or pep talks will address an executive functioning issue as it is usually not possible for the autistic person to just change how they do things.

A useful way to address executive functioning issues is to build strategies around the issue which enable your daughter to do the thing she finds difficult. Strategies tend to work best when the autistic person themselves is involved in working out a plan which will help address the issue. Your daughter may need support and guidance with coming up with a plan but there are usually ways around executive functioning issues. Things which might assist for time management include using scheduling apps, a system of reminders, working with parents or trusted friends to give a reminder or series of reminders when an exam or deadline is approaching.

Accessing support services

Some student disability support services are very helpful and other less so. It is usually a good idea to link in with them as they can provide practical assistance and also link your daughter in with other non-disability specific services on campus. In many places, students are eligible for discounted health, transport and other services.

Some students do not want to access disability support services, particularly if they are self-conscious about their autism diagnosis and worry their colleagues much judge them. However, many adjustments and supports can be done discreetly. A lot of people access different services now and having diagnostic 'labels' may be less stigmatising than it might have been in the past. As always, your daughter needs to be driving or at least involved in decisions around accessing student support services and other supports.

Perfectionism

Perfectionism is a form of anxiety and fear of failure and despite seeming to be a good problem to have, it can be damaging. Perfectionism can turn a high distinction essay into a failing grade if the student cannot part with it until it is 'perfect'. Perfectionism can be misinterpreted as a lack of engagement or interest, but it is quite the opposite.

There are a few strategies which can help with perfectionism. These include working on the root causes, anxiety and fear of making a mistake. These are things which may be best addressed with a mental health or autism professional. In practical terms, perfectionism can be challenged through giving the student some perspective. Often, although not always, perfectionists have the potential for high achievement. If you can contrast their worry that their work isn't perfect with the knowledge that most people would be very happy to submit an essay which will get a pass or a credit grade. A kind of reality check can also be used around their work where they have the question posed as to what the outcome would actually be, if their work was not perfect. This strategy can work very well around perfectionism in employment as well.

Exams: revision, anxiety, etc.

Some autistic people never study and walk into an exam and get a high distinction. This is not true for everyone though. Many autistic people struggle with exams for a variety of reasons. One of the biggest issues is anxiety. Even if the person knows the topic really well, nerves can result in a poor result. Autistic people often worry a few steps further ahead than their non-autistic colleagues. So while a non-autistic student might worry about failing an exam and having to repeat the subject their autistic colleague might worry they will fail the exam, then have to leave their course and never get a job as a result and be poor and miserable forever. This makes concern around exam results a bit more understandable!

Anxiety is the basis for difficulties in a number of other areas. There are a few ways to address this. The young person can do some work with a psychologist or other therapist to help manage their anxiety. Some people find using medication – for some a short or other a longer time – helpful. Things like mindfulness can be helpful with a range of psychological issues, including anxiety and many people benefit from physical exercise and / or yoga. Some of these strategies can have positive impacts on other areas of their life.

There are a lot of supports available for autistic students. Many education institutions provide a more autism friendly way of doing exams – often in a private room or in a smaller group and with breaks if the student needs them. These sorts of measures can help with the more practical issues of exams - sensory, difficulties a room full of people doing distracting things or a need to stop and regroup for a bit. The best preparation for an exam or other stressful situation (e.g. job interview) is preparation. Knowing as much as you can and understanding what the environment will be like for the test can alleviate a lot of issues. Preparation for an exam does not just include study but also; knowing what the room the exam is in will look like, how many people will be in the room, what the expectations are, what happens if your pen runs out of ink, how long you will be in the exam for, what to do if you finish before everyone else, those kinds of issues. Preparation may help remove a lot of the anxiety around the exam and leave the young person to focus on the content of the exam.

POST SCHOOL STUDYING TIPS FOR AUTISTIC SPECTRUM YOUNG WOMEN

OVERVIEW OF FURTHER EDUCATION TRANSITIONS

Undertaking post-school study is often a great opportunity to build skills for a career. Further education differs greatly from high school with the students there being more likely to be genuinely interested in study and learning, rather than having to be and resenting being there. Further education can be a positive step into adulthood and many people meet good friends at college.

Further education is a big step for autistic young women. If they have entered further education directly after high school, there are a number of significant differences. Students are treated as adults, learning needs to be done more independently and the dynamics of relationships with academic staff are very different to a student - teacher interaction in school. University or college is a big place - physically and socially. There is rarely follow up for late assignments from academic staff and the level of support which students have in school is significantly decreased at university. There is an expectation of independence and many students live out of home. For autistic women there can be some huge advantages of university compared to high school but also some big challenges.

Some of the positives of further education include:

- ▶ Reward for academic achievement
- ▶ Some lecturers being approachable and supportive around mental health and Autism-related issues
- ▶ Being treated as an independent adult
- ▶ Being appreciated by student colleagues for being an academic achiever, unlike in high school where being as academic achiever can contribute to bullying
- ▶ A large variety of subjects can be available
- ▶ The opportunity to achieve and succeed

Some of the drawbacks in further education include:

- ▶ There is not always a lot of support around autism. Student disability services tend to be less 'hands-on' than autism and disability services and supports in school
- ▶ While in high school students may have a home room teacher and other staff who oversee their health and wellbeing, academic staff in further education generally don't do this.
- ▶ Schools tend to report difficulties a student is having to their parents. However, in further education the academic staff do not usually have any

relationship with parents or other support people and deal directly with the student themselves. For autistic women who may struggle to articulate their distress and / or ask for help, this can result in difficulties.

- ▸ The coursework can be hard to keep up with. The structure of work in further education is often quite different to that at school. The transition to independent learning can be very difficult.

- ▸ Exams are often the main form of assessment in university courses. While some autistic people are great at exams, for many the anxiety surrounding exams can be devastating and result in poor performance. They may score poorly or fail, not because they don't know the subject but because of the pressures in exams.

- ▸ There may be no introductions to other students at the start of the course or subjects. For autistic women with social phobia or anxiety this can be very stressful and proactively introducing themselves to fellow students can be more difficult than the coursework. This can lead to autistic women feeling socially isolated and without friends where other students are forming friendships and socializing.

Further education can be an amazing opportunity for autistic women, but it can also be incredibly challenging. The education attainment rates for autistic people are significantly lower for autistic people, than the general population. For this reason, providing support to autistic people in further education is essential. In contrast a number of autistic women thrive in further education and obtain a number of degrees.

Question:

Should I do more study after I leave school? What is the point?

Advice and Guidance:

Further study is often a pathway to employment opportunities, Research shows that the higher level of education that someone attains, the greater their chance of finding work which is suitable for them. Given that autistic women can struggle in the labour market, further education is very important. Even if you do a course which doesn't relate directly to the career or job that you want, having any kind of further education qualifications is a good thing. To an employer, the fact a potential job seeker can complete a course of study is a good indication that they have the necessary skills and commitment to timelines to succeed in employment.

Question:

I really love animals, but I find it very hard to talk to people. I have a place to study vet science at a local college. Will I be able to manage at college?

Advice and Guidance:

Social interactions with other humans is part of face to face further study and it might be challenging for you to undertake the course in this format. However, you can build in some strategies for managing the need to interact with the human participants. It is OK to be studious and focus on your studies, but it might be worth preparing some responses to requests for social engagement. In terms of socializing outside of class, there is no rule saying you need to interact with your peers. They might think you are being 'rude' if you do not socialize at all. Some people don't mind being viewed as rude or anti-social. but others are more sensitive and feel criticized by these reactions. One way to address this is to tell your peers that you are autistic and that you have difficulties socializing, though that choice is not for everyone.

Another strategy is to focus on the outcome of your course, potentially getting a job in the field of veterinary science and working with animals. Focusing on the outcome or objective of what you are doing can be a great motivator which can enable you to navigate through difficulties in the relatively short term. If you choose to study online instead be aware that this can pose challenges too.

A lot of people, including neurotypical people, are not comfortable socializing and prefer to keep to themselves, this is perfectly OK. However, you may choose to be brave and try going to an event or activity with classmates. If you do this, even though it may be difficult and overwhelming at first, you may well find that you do get some enjoyment out of this. If this is the case, be prepared to feel 'all people out' afterwards. Once you take some time to yourself to recover, you will feel ok again. You may then choose to be social with others once or twice a week and have time for yourself and/or your interests and passions, the rest of the time. However, there is no reason you won't be able to succeed in your course.

Question:

I need some practical tips to make going to college/university easier for me. I am an autistic spectrum young woman. How can I make sure I don't drop out or fail my course?

Advice and Guidance:

It can be helpful to put in place strategies which support you to continue studying. You can use services like the university disability support center to help address any issues you may have with studying. This can include assistance taking notes in lectures and putting in place some strategies around exams or other forms of assessment.

If you are happy at university and enjoy your course you are less likely to want to leave. You may find the subject you were really interested in is not in fact to your liking or does not cover the subject matter in a way that you enjoy or expected. It is hard to be happy at university if you do not enjoy the coursework. In this situation it may be worth changing your degree or elective subjects. Changing courses requires completing some paperwork and is often quite easy, as long as you meet the entrance requirements for that course. Sometimes, we can find that we really enjoy something we did not anticipate, which is why some of the wide ranging first year courses can help us to choose a subject to continue more in-depth.

If you have difficulties with some of the practical elements of study; getting to university, sensory issues in lectures, writing essays, having the right text books or journal articles at the right time, then the best way to address these is to find some strategies which help you overcome the particular issue you are having. For example, for sensory issues removing or compensating for the cause of distress is the best option. You can tell your lecturer/tutor about the issue that is causing the distress. This is an area where the disability services unit can probably help. For every issue there is a workaround or strategy, you may just need support to work out what this is. Find what works for you and do it.

Another issue for autistic students is perfectionism.

This is a mixture of anxiety and fear of failure and can be debilitating, especially at university. A good strategy for perfectionism is considering perspective. "If I submit the essay and it is not perfect, what will the impact be?" "If I make the essay perfect but submit it late, what will the outcome be?"

Perfectionism is useful in some situations, such as calculating bridge strength or brain surgery, but problematic in others, such as essay writing. It really is ok to not write a perfect essay, it is much more important to submit your assignments on time as there are usually grade penalties for each day that an assignment is late.

Question:

I just started a course at university. Should I tell people I am autistic or not?

Advice and Guidance:

This is entirely up to you. The decision as to whether to let others know you are Autistic and what that means is a personal one and will vary according to the situation. Some positives of telling others about your autism include that you can access support services which require you to have a diagnosis and you do not need to keep a 'secret'. Positives around disclosing also include that you are demonstrating you accept your autism as part of you and do not view it as shameful or something that needs hiding, which can help you to feel more self-confident. You can also become a role model for other autistic people if you are willing to talk about your autism. This can help you to meet other autistic students, some of whom you may find you want to become friends with.

Whether or not you are open about your autism depends on a range of factors. Firstly, you need to decide whether to tell anyone. The second consideration is what to say about your autism, do you go into detail or just mention it in passing? The third consideration is about when to say anything. Will you mention your autism when you apply for the course, when you find out you have been accepted, when you commence study or when you have been at university for a while? The next considerations are who to tell. Do you tell your lecturers and tutors, your colleagues, administration staff? The final consideration is what do you think the impact of talking about your autism is and why do you want to or not want to? You can consider these things and then work out a strategy or plan around talking about autism in your course.

Some people will stick to their plan but for others it simply provides guidance which can be adapted depending on the situation. For example, you may want to tell a tutor you are autistic, but they might say something ableist or which demonstrates they are ableist (think people with disabilities are less than other people). This may well impact on your decision. Conversely you may not want to disclose and then a lecturer might talk about their autistic child, partner or relative in a respectful way which will encourage you to feel safe telling them that you are autistic.

It is important to be aware that your autism is nothing to be ashamed of and in a better word nobody would feel the need to hide their diagnosis. Issues around disclosure only exist due to ableist attitudes and negative stereotypes and/or prejudice around autism. So, your strategy around disclosure is essentially a strategy for managing potentially ableist and disrespectful attitudes in society, or accessing support to help you succeed, rather than to change anything in you.

Question:

I have been away from study for a while. How do I prepare for taking a university course?

Advice and Guidance:

Completing a course in further education requires a number of skills, many of which are intangible. Your motivation to do the course is probably the key skill required to succeed in further education. If you are enthusiastic and want to learn and have a goal attached to your course, it will be infinitely easier than if you are there because someone else expects you to be. For example, I completed my initial teaching degree because I really wanted to be a teacher and knew that it was a job that would enable me to work anywhere in the world, which was important to me.

For autistic people though motivation alone may not always be enough. There can be challenges and barriers which make activities like education and work difficult for autistic people. The new environment, university or other further education environments can be challenging. Some of the unfamiliar elements may include:

▸ New physical environment

▸ New ways of learning

▸ Exams and assignments

▸ Different people – and often having to meet new people

▸ New/different ways of thinking and speaking

▸ Using different technology or tools

▸ Different sorts of social groups

▸ Independent learning – less direct support than

school or work

For autistic children, things like social stories often help manage such a transition. As an adult, a social story might seem pitched at the wrong level of maturity, but the principle can translate to adult life. For adults, a mental road map can be used to address new situations. A more practical road map/plan can step out things like the physical environment of the campus, the physical trip there; whether you drive, walk or take public transport to university.

Autistic adults are sometimes, but not always, engaged in the subject they are studying and are often, but not always, very proficient academically. However, this may not translate into good grades if they have severe anxiety around exams or struggle with assignments. Autistic students may be seen as underperforming or disengaged when in fact they need support to manage their challenges and find strategies to enable them to demonstrate their skills or knowledge in the course. Sometimes the supports needed are really simple, such as having a colour coded timetable with a map of the campus. At other times supports may be more all-encompassing, such as having a reader/writer to facilitate access to assignments.

Question:

How can I find a peer group or friends in further education?

Advice and Guidance:

It can sometimes be easier to find a peer group or friends in further education than at school. As people mature they often become less embarrassed by seeming 'odd' than they did as teenagers and are students in further education are usually more open and respectful of the kinds of perceived differences which can result in autistic teens being ostracized in their teens. Students in further education often choose a narrower group of subjects than in school. For autistic students this can mean they are focusing on their area of interest and their fellow students are as well so they all presumably share that interest. Shared interests are often the base of long-lasting friendships and many people keep the friends they made at college/university throughout life.

Many autistic women find making friends at university or further education considerably easier than in school. There are clubs and societies in many further education settings. These clubs range from cultural to political to activity based, and many interests are covered. In some universities there are disability and / or autism students' clubs and associations. These can be a great starting point for friendships and peer groups. You can also set up a club around your particular interest if one does not already exist.

Further education can be an isolating experience for some people. Some courses have a lot of elective topics, so students do not have a core group of peers. Many autistic women find it hard to 'break in' to social settings where they don't know the people well. They may want friends but not have the confidence to start a conversation. When I started university, I had a number of lectures in large groups of over 100 students and was always sitting by myself on the edge of the group. However, after I joined a lesbian and gay student group, I felt more confident sitting with some of the other students from that group in these large lectures.

Question:

I have been told that there are lots of hidden curriculum / unwritten rules in further education. How do I find out what these are?

Advice and Guidance:

Communication in the non-autistic world comes with a lot of 'hidden curriculum'/ unwritten rules, which most non-autistic people seem to innately understand but which leave autistic folks metaphorically scratching their heads and wondering how that magic trick worked!

Further education is no exception. Most situations; socializing, attending lectures or tutorials, study etc. have these kinds of unwritten rules attached. 'Small talk' is a kind of unwritten rule which non-autistic people tend to use in order to introduce a conversation or interaction. Whilst they may be talking about topics such as the weather or what they did on their weekend, the subject matter is in fact irrelevant, the talk is simply designed to start an interaction. However, an autistic person who talks about the weather tends to do so out of a genuine interest in meteorological occurrences! As you can probably imagine this can lead to some conversations where the non-autistic and autistic participants might find one another confusing!

In further education, a lot of the unwritten social rules focus on activities like parties and relationships as well as discussions around grades and coursework. There are also rules around such areas as lending money / paying for meals, carpooling and behaviour at parties. Sex and relationships come with a whole slew of unwritten rules which can be very confusing and upsetting of those not 'in the know.'

Autistic women have a few options around unwritten rules and the various hidden curricula in further education. Some autistic people will learn how to work as closely within the hidden curriculum of non-autistic people as possible, others might explain at the outset that they are autistic and can find social 'rules' confusing. The latter tends to be preferable for people who are open about being autistic, but some people will be more comfortable trying to learn relevant aspects of non-autistic 'culture.' The main consideration around the hidden curriculum of non-autistic communication is really to know it exists and what sort of activities and behaviours are as a result of this. It is then possible to learn to navigate it in a way which is effective for each individual.

Question:

I have heard that further education campuses are dangerous for autistic young women. How can I keep myself safe?

Advice and Guidance:

Further education is very different from school. Students are adults and are treated as adults. Activities like drinking alcohol and having sex are acceptable for university/college students whereas in high school these things were discouraged and, in some cases, illegal. Many students in further education live away from their childhood homes and sometimes on campus among other young people. An autistic woman in further education will almost certainly be exposed to some activities which did not take place at school or which only took place on occasions such as a party.

There is not usually a lot of education about self-protection, but it is an essential skill. Self-protection refers to being able to avoid dangerous situations and know what to do to get you out of potentially dangerous situations, particularly around sexual or aggressive/violent activity. This is particularly important for autistic women because autistic women can be very trusting and naive. They may find it hard to imagine anyone being abusive and take everything said to them on face value. They may also be unaware of non-verbal cues which non-autistic people know apparently instinctively. This can lead to being in situations that become dangerous but being unaware of the upcoming danger.

There are things like physical self-defense courses which can be helpful but a lot of the understanding of self-protection comes from understanding what a risky situation looks like. Assertiveness is another important part of set protection. Some women on the autism spectrum can know that a situation is risky and want to get away but go along with the abuser for fear of challenging the abuser and making it worse.

It is important to teach your daughter:

▸ What the law says, in regard to sexual behaviour – what is consensual and what isn't

▸ A list of examples of potentially risky situations and how to avoid them

▸ Actions to look out for - e.g. a man she has just offering to buy alcoholic drinks for her or someone trying to entice her into their house under the guise of seeing something interesting

▸ Teaching a selection of assertive 'no!' responses to different situations

▸ Strategies for safety like going to a party or pub with a female friend

▸ Information on advisers not necessarily looking 'creepy'

▸ Ensuring she knows that the only person with the

right to decide what happens with her body is her

▸ Physical self-defence

It might seem alarmist or overly paranoid to worry about these issues but a large portion of women and autistic women particularly, are victim to sexual predators and a new environment like further education with new people and different 'rules' around social behaviour, in combination with rapists' seemingly intuitive way to find a 'soft target' means self-protection is essential for young autistic women.

Question:

What can universities do to assist autistic women students?

Advice and Guidance:

Universities and other education provides can support autistic women in a variety of ways, including:

▸ Provide more targeted disability support services. Some education providers do this but in some providers disability student services only provide very limited assistance, such as note-taking in lectures.

▸ More visible diversity policies and leadership around disability

▸ Promote clubs and societies for autistic students and / or students with disability

▸ Provide peer mentoring programs for students (not just students with disability but all students who need or want it)

▸ Have an orientation programme which isn't just

about 'beer and bands' but which helps students get to know their peers, tutors/lecturers and the physical environment of the campus prior to starting the course

- ► Build understanding about autism with lecturers and administrative staff so they can help address any issues and understand the needs of autistic students
- ► Offering social and support groups for students and staff on the Autism spectrum and/or with disability or mental illness.

THE WORLD OF WORK FOR AUTISTIC SPECTRUM WOMEN

It can be hard for autistic women to feel comfortable and supported in the workplace. This chapter will explore how to manage looking for work and being employed, social expectations at work, challenges which may arise and strategies for succeeding in the workplace.

Question:

Please can I have some practical tips for applying for jobs and attending interviews?

Advice and Guidance:

There are some strategies which can assist to succeed in recruitment processes and job interviews. These include:

▸ Talk to friends and / family members about their experience of applying for jobs. It can be particularly helpful to talk to other autistic people about their experiences – what worked, what didn't and if they have any useful tips.

▸ Have the attitude when you apply that you do not yet have the job. So if you do not get it, you will have lost nothing but if you get it that it will be a big bonus. This approach can help to address some of the anxiety around job applications.

▸ If such a thing is available where you live, consider going through a disability or autism recruitment scheme. If help is there, you can make use of it.

▸ Job interviews can be extremely challenging for autistic people. While some workplaces use alternative sorts of recruitment processes, being selected for most jobs will involve an interview.

As with any activity which is anxiety-provoking, with job interviews preparation is the key. Some strategies for job interviews include:

▸ Research the company the position is in. You can demonstrate your understanding of the company based on this research in the interview. This can be done through some targeted Googling.

▸ Many interview panels ask applicants if they have a question at the end of the interview. They are usually looking for the applicant to demonstrate their understanding of the work of the company rather than asking what the salary or hours will be! You can use your research on the company to develop such a question.

▸ Practice interview technique with a friend, your partner or a family member or in front of the mirror. Think about what questions the panel might ask and what your responses will be and have a practice interview. This can help you to feel more confident and prepared for the actual interview.

▸ If possible, talk to friends and family about their

experiences of job interviews and what worked, what didn't work and what they found helpful.

▸ Remember that job interviews favour confident extroverts and most people – including non-autistic people – are not confident extroverts and will be feeling uncomfortable at the interview too. Being aware of this can help you feel less anxious.

Question:

I really need some practical self-advocacy strategies for use in the workplace. How can I get the support that I need to do my job well?

Advice and Guidance:

When an autistic person joins the workplace, there is often a gap in their understanding of autism and the understanding of autism among their managers and colleagues. Advocacy can help bridge this gap and challenge unhelpful assumptions and misunderstandings in the workplace. Advocacy can include such activities as:

▸ Telling your immediate supervisor about your autism and what it means for you

▸ Asking for causes of sensory distress to be changed to accommodate your needs

▸ Giving presentations on autism to colleagues and the workplace or arranging for another autistic speaker to do this

▸ Simply being 'out' as autistic at work

▸ Challenging ableism or the discrimination in the workplace

▸ Supporting other autistic colleagues

- Being part of networks for staff with disability in your workplace
- Speaking up if injustice is being done to you and another autistic person at work.

Advocating for yourself at work is a great thing to do if you can. You know yourself and your needs better than anyone. The best person to talk about autism in is the autistic person themselves. However, this can be difficult to do, especially in a new job.

Self-advocacy is often the best way to explain to people at your workplace about what autism is, what autism means to you and what supports you might need to do your job well. Sometimes non-autistic people are unaware that something they do might cause you anxiety. For example, people whispering at work might trigger social anxiety but the people whispering may not realize it is upsetting. A lot of helpful self-advocacy happens when an autistic person explains to their colleagues and managers what autism means to them and what they can do to assist. Explaining needs such as strategies to address sensory issues or discussion around social communication misunderstandings can be helpful and is a practical way to advocate for yourself.

The best advocacy is often based on shared understanding. Sharing your knowledge and experience of autism with your managers and colleagues can be an amazing opportunity to build that knowledge. It can be helpful to look at some information on self-advocacy to help you advocate for yourself. Getting involved with advocacy groups such as the Autistic Self-Advocacy Network or Autism Women's Association can be really helpful. You can also join in on conversations in online autism advocacy groups and get some assistance and pointers around advocating at work from others in a similar situation to you.

You can request a friend or an advocate from an autism advocacy organisation to talk to your managers and colleagues if you are not comfortable doing so yourself. If you have established a good working relationship with your supervisor or another manager, you can ask them to speak to your colleagues on your behalf, making sure you have seen / heard and approved what they talk about before they do so. It is often helpful to be present for the conversation with your colleagues to enable you to explain or clarify anything.

Question:

I love my job, but I really hate the social expectations of drinks after work on a Friday and regularly get togethers to eat lunch with colleagues. Will I lose my job if I don't join in?

Advice and Guidance:

Social expectations in the workplace can be challenging.

The short answer to this question is no. Essentially there should be no consequences to your job security for not attending social functions or eating lunch with colleagues. However, not joining in can result in you feeling isolated at work and may have an impact on how your managers and colleagues view you. Social interaction at work is part of the hidden curriculum in the workplace, unwritten rules that non-autistic people usually understand but which autistic people can struggle to understand or be aware of. It can be helpful to have some strategies and responses, so colleagues understand you are not being rude or unfriendly by not joining in social activities, just looking out for yourself.

Regarding eating lunch with your colleagues, quite a lot of people will eat lunch alone, not just autistics. Introverted and shy people who are not autistic may also eat lunch alone at work. It is perfectly OK to do so. If somebody asks you to join them and you don't want to, work out a script to explain you don't want to in a way which is respectful to them and which works for you. It might be along the lines of 'I need some quiet time' or 'I prefer to eat alone. It is just something I do.'

In terms of after work drinks, it is unlikely that your entire team will be there. Some people do not drink alcohol for a number of reasons and other people struggle with socializing. There are two basic tactics for communicating that you don't wish to attend after work drinks. The first option involves truthfully talking about the reasons you don't wish to attend, either with or without mentioning your autism. If you are 'out' as autistic at work, you could explain that socializing outside of work with groups of colleagues is overwhelming for you and that you like your colleagues but find social situations difficult. If you are not 'out' about your autism at work, you can still talk about the genuine reasons you are not comfortable socializing. You can talk about being introverted or shy.

As with many hidden curriculum social 'rules' non-autistic people have their own expectations governing social behaviour. You can follow this rule if you like. It basically involves making an excuse about why you are not attending work drinks. These reasons may not be entirely true but in this context that is OK. Some excuses you might use are:

- ► 'I'm very tired'
- ► 'I have something else on after work'
- ► 'I don't really feel like going out' or
- ► 'I don't drink alcohol.'

If you use this strategy, while excuses can be not entirely true, they should be vague and not about anything terrible, like 'my partner was in a car accident.' This strategy is certainly not for everyone, but some autistic people find it helpful, particularly those who are not 'out' at work.

Question:

After I have had a job for about six months I either quit or I start to get really anxious and stressed. Is this normal?

Advice and Guidance:

This can be quite common for autistic women, although it has not been formally researched. Anecdotal evidence suggests that this happens for one of three main reasons:

- ▶ Having mastered the job, you are now bored, but do not necessarily recognize the feelings as boredom and instead are interpreting them as anxiety or stress. Or you quit because the challenge has gone, and you are bored!

- ▶ You are anxious and stressed because of possible conflict in the workplace. It can take up to six months for many of us to start to be aware of and start developing an understanding of the workplace hierarchy and other hidden curriculum areas at work. Many of us really dislike conflict and so when we get anxious or stressed about real or even potential conflict we can try to avoid it, which when it is at work often means quitting.

- ▶ You are being bullied by your colleagues and/or line manager. Sadly, this is a very common occurrence for autistic women in the workplace. It seems that non-autistic people find it difficult to classify and thus respond appropriately to people who are quite different to them. Even the way that we stand, or dress can mark us out as different, no matter what the level of job that we are doing. Many autistics in this situation feel that they cannot quit because they need the income. However, they can become more and more anxious and/or stressed as time goes on. This stress and/or anxiety can contribute to increased shutdowns and/or meltdowns, which unfortunately can lead to being fired/let go. The fear of this happening can lead some autistics to quit.

If you are in situation one, it is better to get another job before quitting as it is much harder to get a new job when you are out of work that it is when you are employed. Other options are freelancing, contract/temp work or self-employment in an area that you are currently interested in.

If you are in situation two, your anxiety and/or stress can be decreased by working through your fears and what exactly is bothering you with a trusted friend or family member. Sometimes we can get upset about things that we perceive as unfair, but which our colleagues have no issue with. It can help to be aware of this and then to make informed decisions about whether or not you want to continue working there. Some people can talk to their line manager or supervisor about any issues and then resolve them, however, other people find this difficult or know that this will not help.

Again, if you can get another job before resigning, that will make job hunting easier.

If you are in situation three, you can talk to your union representative if you are in a union and ask them to help support you. If you are not in a union, and your line manager is not involved in the bullying, it is worth trying to talk to them. If, however, they are also bullying you, you may choose to make a complaint to an ombudsman or if the bullying is physical in any way, a police complaint. Your mental health is very important, so if this is starting to be impacted seek, professional help via your GP/family doctor. At this point, your anxiety of stress may be so high that you need to take sick leave. If this happens, whilst you are off sick, it would be a good idea to plan how you can find another way to earn a living.

See questions relating to bullying for further advice and guidance.

Question:

What is a good career, and can autistic women have one?

Advice and Guidance:

The notion of a 'good career' is quite a subjective thing. A career which works well for one person will not work well for another. What constitutes a good career is essentially what is good for the individual employee. It is important not to apply some arbitrary criteria based on someone else's needs. Your view of what is a good career will most likely change over time. For example, when you are a young person, your requirement from employment might be a higher wage so you can set yourself up. If later on you want to have children, your criteria for a good career might be more focused on the ability to have flexible arrangements around child care and school hours.

▸ Ideally a job which most people would consider a 'good career' should provide a number of benefits including:

- Working hours which are suitable and allow you to do what you need to outside of work
- A salary that covers all the employee's regular expenses and allows some capacity for saving
- A working environment free form bullying and harassment including ableism, racism, sexism, homophobia, transphobia and other forms of discrimination
- The opportunity for career advancement and development for all employees who aspire to and are capable of working at a higher level, regardless of characteristics such as autism
- A work environment where people are friendly and accepting
- Conditions which support the employee's life outside of work (leave, superannuation, health insurance etc)
- A safe workplace - both physical and mental
- Ability to access genuine recourse if a grievance occurs
- Access to flexible work arrangements for parents and others who need this (such as those with caring responsibilities).

Most workplaces will not have all these elements, but they are good practices and anyone working at such a workplace would be supported to achieve their career goals.

On top of these considerations, there are some career needs which may be more sought after for autistic women. These could include things like flexible arrangements with leave or part-time hours, so you can have one or more days a week to have time out. Autistic women might have concerns in the workplace that non-autistic people are unaware of such as sensory considerations and a quiet workspace. However, there is no 'perfect' career which suits all autistic women. Each autistic woman is different and will benefit from different arrangements and conditions at work.

So, the short answer to this question is that there is no one good career for autistic women but that autistic women can have a good career providing it supports them and meets their needs, at whichever stage of life they are in.

Question:

I am autistic, and I have children, but I find that I do not have enough energy to cope with full time work and being a mum. How do other people manage it all?

Advice and Guidance:

It can be very hard to raise children and work full-time. For autistic women, balancing full-time work and raising children can be particularly challenging. Autistic women may struggle getting adequate sleep, they may have children who have high support needs, and/or they may have mental health issues like anxiety and depression, which impact on their ability to have enough energy and stamina to get through the working week, perform well at work and care for their children.   Many women with children work part-time or use flexible work practices. Some employers support mothers of children living at home through using flexible work arrangements but not all employers do. The workplaces which offer flexible work arrangements are not confined to one industry, but they are often professional or corporate sorts of employers.

Flexible work arrangements can include a wide range of practices including job-sharing (where two employees work part-time in the same position), part-time hours or arrangements where an employee works during school hours. One consideration around working part-time is the impact on your income, so it is a good idea to work out your budget prior to going part-time. If you work in an organization which has a Human Resources area, sometimes known as People and Culture, staff there can assist with calculations showing what your income will be for part-time hours. In many countries, employees have a legal entitlement to access part-time work where it is available.

You may also want to address any difficulties you have outside of work impacting on your energy levels. This could include working out some strategies to aid sleep, respite for your children - or you - and putting in place some effective strategies around mental health to enable you to function better.

Question:

What happens if I have a meltdown at work?

Advice and Guidance:

For many autistic employees, having a meltdown at work is the ultimate fear, especially for people who have not told managers or colleagues they are autistic. While it is very helpful to learn and use some de-escalation strategies which help let the pressure and overload out before it becomes a meltdown, this is not always possible.

Many autistic people, and particularly adults, will have a fair idea of their triggers and what sorts of things are likely to lead to a meltdown. If this is the case for you and you feel a meltdown building up while you are at work, the best thing to do is take yourself somewhere quiet and preferably private and let out whatever you need to let out.

Unfortunately, this is not always possible, and you may have a meltdown during work with colleagues and managers watching. While you are likely to be incredibly stressed by this, there are some strategies to manage it. It is important when looking at meltdowns to be aware that for non-autistic people who have not witnessed one and do not understand it, it may seem like poor behaviour, a mental health issue or a tantrum. So, if you do have a meltdown at work then the first thing you all need to do after you recover and are able to, is to explain what happened.

If you are 'out' about your autism at work, it is likely to be much easier to explain a meltdown in the context of your autism. You can explain that autistic people experience overload and meltdowns can occur. It is important to stress that it is not intentional or poor behaviour and that, by the time the overload becomes a meltdown, you do not have control over it. If you have not talked to your managers and colleagues about your autism, you can still explain a meltdown in relation to your own experience. In fact, a meltdown at work for somebody who has kept their autism a secret at work may be an opportunity to think about whether it is a good idea to tell staff about your autism.

Whatever positive strategies you use, there will be people who judge your professionalism and level of competence harshly due to the meltdown. This is not your fault and if you have given them a clear explanation of what happened and how you will try to address it in future, then you have done all you can do.

A meltdown at work can be seen in terms of risk management. There are two types of risk: the likelihood a meltdown will occur and what the consequences might be if it does. A good plan for managing risks involves measures which act on both the likelihood of a meltdown occurring and also measures which act on the consequence if it does occur. You can use a table like the one below to manage your meltdown risks:

Measure	Addresses likelihood	Addresses consequence	Impact of measures on the risk of meltdown and its consequences
Identify triggers - sensory, emotional, social.	Yes	No	Helps address overload before it becomes a meltdown.
Practice de-escalation straggles.	Yes	No	Should avoid entirely or lessen the magnitude of the meltdown.
Talk to you supervisor / manager / colleagues about what a meltdown is and what causes it.	Yes	Yes	This should help people you work with understand meltdowns better and allow you to be more understanding if overload or stressors eventuate. This could in fact help you to avoid overload in the first place.

Measure	Addresses likelihood	Addresses consequence	Impact of measures on the risk of meltdown and its consequences
Establish a positive relationship with your supervisor.	Yes	Yes	Can mean you feel - and are - supported at work and issues which might cause overload can be addressed early If a meltdown occurs your supervisor can help you and your colleagues to understand what happened.

Measure	Addresses likelihood	Addresses consequence	Impact of measures on the risk of meltdown and its consequences
Develop a communication strategy for if a meltdown occurs.	No	Yes	This will help enable you to discuss and explain a meltdown if it occurs. It can also help to minimise the stress of a meltdown in the workplace because you do not need to come up with a response right away but can refer back to this.

Meltdowns in and of themselves are not illegal and often will not breach the code of conduct in your workplace. However, they can be confronting for those witnessing them. In some instances, autistic people can become self-destructive or aggressive during a meltdown. If this happens to you and your actions breach the code of conduct at your workplace or the law, you may be subject to legal consequence or performance and conduct procedures. While autistic people do not want or intend to have a meltdown, this is not widely understood. Where possible, building understanding with your supervisor and/or colleagues of what a meltdown is, what it isn't and why it occurs is a helpful strategy in the workplace.

Question:

I really struggle with the work hierarchy. Why do I have to talk to senior managers differently to colleagues? It's not like they are any smarter!

Advice and Guidance:

The function of the hierarchy in a workplace is usually to ensure decisions are made by a person who is sufficiently qualified to make them. The hierarchy is also used to ensure staff members are being managed by somebody with the appropriate expertise to do so. In an ideal world all managers and supervisors would have the required expertise and personal qualities to enable them to support their staff to do their jobs well and would make reasonable and wise decisions relating to the company. In reality some managers are promoted beyond their level of competence and others have poor interpersonal skills with staff.

The hierarchy at work does not mean someone is better or worse than anyone else, even if that is the impression some managers might give. Managers and staff need to treat each other with the same level of respect and courtesy. However, this does not mean all managers are professional or courteous.

As autistics we can be acutely aware of where managers are deficient. However, there are some unwritten social rules around dealing with difficult or incompetent managers. Unless the manager is doing something illegal or against the code of conduct for your workplace, pointing out their failings to them or their manager is more likely to impact negatively on you, particularly if you do it in front of colleagues. Even taking the manager aside and giving them polite constructive criticism could be misinterpreted.

Basically, when you agree to work for an organisation

one of the things which is expected is that you carry out reasonable and lawful instructions from managers (reasonable in this instance meaning lawful and within the policy of the organization you are working for). Even if your manager or a senior executive makes a decision or gives a direction which you see as unwise or misinformed, it is best not to criticize them publicly or directly about it.

If you are promoted to a higher level in the hierarchy at your workplace, it is a good idea to find out what differences that will mean in your work, will you be supervising staff? If so, is there learning and development available which you can access around managing staff well, so that you can be a good manager?

Question:

How do I know whether I'm doing a good job or not if my manager doesn't tell me? Is it OK to ask for feedback?

Advice and Guidance:

Different managers have different approaches to their job, some managers will give frequent feedback and others will give very little. It can be anxiety-provoking to wait for your manager to tell you if you are doing a good job or not. If you start a new job you may want more feedback initially to make sure you are doing a good job. Autistic people can find it hard to see their work objectively so may have no idea if they are doing a good job or not. You may need assurance from your manager that your work is of a good standard to a greater extent than non-autistic employees.

It is usually OK to ask a manager for feedback on your work. However, this is one of those areas where being too persistent can actually become counter-productive and mean your manager is likely to become irritated. What constitutes a reasonable number of requests for feedback can differ between managers and also change depending on how long you have been working for that manager. Some general tips include:

- Discuss your need for feedback with your manager early on in the work relationship. Explain that you may need reassurance. Set the boundaries and expectations around asking for feedback. If it helps you to actually write a list of rules around the process of asking for feedback, do that.

- You can ask your supervisor for a regular catch up session to discuss what you are working on and to discuss your performance. Many people do this.

- Remember that no feedback will most likely mean you are doing an adequate or a good job. Most managers will raise issues with their employees if they are doing anything wrong. So if your manager has not raised an issue about your work, you are probably doing OK.

- Aim not to ask for performance feedback frequently (such as more than one a week).

- If you have a friendship sort of relationship with your manager you can usually safely assume they are happy with your work. Managers who are friends may well assume that you understand your performance is OK and that they would speak to you about your performance if it was not.

- Work out some strategies for managing anxiety and practice being patient.

Question:

My supervisor is always talking down to me and it is really difficult to do my job. She doesn't always let me take annual leave even though nobody else has their leave denied. Is she a bully?

Advice and Guidance:

Workplace bullying does occur and it can be as traumatizing and invalidating as any other kind of bullying, Being bullied at work has the added issue that it is often difficult to leave your job to escape the bullying behaviour as you need the income and it may be hard to find another job. It is important to understand that sometimes a perception of bullying relates to a manager doing their job of managing their staff but in a way that seems too harsh. It can be unclear what are usual management activities and what is bullying. This can cause you to question your perception of the situation.   The situation described here around leave could be interpreted as bullying behaviour or as a manager doing what they need to do in order to get the work done. However, despite there being a lot of grey areas and uncertainty around workplace bullying, if your perception is that you are being bullied, the problem behaviour needs to be addressed.

In some countries, bullying in the workplace is illegal and there are procedures available to address the issue through courts and tribunals. However, following that path can be stressful and expensive. It can result in the person who raises the complaint being discriminated against further, which is totally unfair but can happen. Some ways you can approach the inappropriate behaviour of others in the workplace include:

▶ Talking to the person and expressing that their behaviour is inappropriate and upsetting, It may be the case that the person doesn't realize the impact of their behaviour. However, this can be incredibly difficult to do and if the manager is hostile and intentionally singling you out for discrimination, this approach is unlikely to be effective.

▶ If your workplace has a human resources area, it may well have measures in place to address discrimination, bullying and harassment. If you are comfortable doing so, you can contact human resources and ask what your options are. if you follow this path it is likely the bully will find out you complained about their behaviour which can be problematic but it may also mean the behaviour is addressed and you may be moved to another area or the bully may be instructed to change their behaviour.

- ▸ Write down, somewhere secure and private, what behaviours from your manager are concerning you. Don't use their name but assign an initial or pseudonym. Write as much detail as you can and put dates and times of events where poor behaviour has occurred as much as possible. If you take action about the bullying, you can show this list to the person investigating the complaint and it will help them determine what course of action would be best to support you and tackle the bullying.

- ▸ If there is a union at your workplace and you are a member, you can talk to your union about the bullying. If taking this path, it is worth noting that your employer may react badly to you for bringing the union in. However, it is your right to seek redress if you need to.

- ▸ If things are really bad and you find you get no support at work and people don't take your complaint of bullying seriously, you can look for another job. This option is best used as a last resort particularly as being bullied isn't your fault. However, in some instances workplace bullying can be very damaging for a person psychologically which can lead suicidal thoughts, depression and extreme anxiety. You need to get out of the situation using whatever it takes if your safety is threatened. It is only a job after all and not worth risking your life for.

Question:

I haven't told my manager or colleagues that I have autism. Should I tell them?

Advice and Guidance:

The decision as to whether you tell your manager or your colleagues that you have an autism is a very personal one. The choice is always up to you and should be made after careful consideration and thought. It can be a good idea to make a strategy around what to say to your employer about your autism as well as when to tell them and how much to discuss.

Autism is nothing to be ashamed of. Therefore, hiding it by not telling anyone is doing yourself a disservice. It is similar to you saying to yourself that you are ashamed of something which is not actually shameful at all, your diagnosis. Despite this, talking about your autism at work with colleagues and managers can be very difficult. It is important to note that if you did not disclose your autism before commencing your job and you then ask for modifications to be made to enable you to do your work, your employer may respond negatively by accusing you of failing to disclose relevant information during the hiring process. This can lead to dismissal in some cases. Check with advocacy groups in your country to see if there would be legal repercussions for you if this was your situation.

It is worth thinking about what you will say about your autism, how much you will tell the employer, who you will tell (colleagues, manager, immediate supervisor etc.). Of these considerations, probably most significant is at what stage you talk about your autism, if you decide to do so. Some people find work through a disability employment service provider or recruitment consultant. In this case there is likely a level of information about your autism provided to your employer already. However, if you apply for a job which isn't through a disability employment service provider you can make a decision about talking about your autism. Consider whether you should tell the employer when you apply, during the interview, then you start the job or after you have been working for a little while and know your colleagues and manager. Knowing who you want to tell is important too. Think about who needs to know and who you are comfortable telling.

If you have told your managers that you are autistic, and something comes up at work that you have trouble with, it makes it that much easier for your managers to help you through it. Also, sometimes you might find something in the workplace is causing you distress, for example, communication differences, loud noises or fluorescent lights. If your manager knows that you are on the autism spectrum it will be that much easier for them to make the necessary adjustments to the work environment to ensure you are happy and productive at work. If you choose not to tell, but circumstances arise at work due to your needs as an autistic person, it might be the time to disclose.

There are some potential drawbacks to discussing your autism with managers or colleagues. Recruitment processes can result in discrimination against an openly autistic employee. While it is illegal to discriminate against people with health conditions and disability in recruitment or employment, in reality it is very difficult to prove that an employer has decided not to hire you because you are autistic. If you took them to court for discrimination in hiring, an employer could just as easily say that they thought you were not suited to the job, even if they actually did discriminate against you.

You can be being 'pigeon-holed' as a staff member with a disability. You may find it hard to be given work in areas which aren't somehow related to disability issues, even if you want to. Your talents and skills may go unused due to assumptions and stereotypes around what autistic people are good at. There is evidence to suggest that staff who identify as having a disability find it harder to progress in their career and get promoted as well.

With all the various pros and cons and different managers and workplaces you might work at, knowing what to say about your autism at work is a difficult decision. It can help to give the issue some serious consideration and determine a strategy to help make the decision when applying for jobs. Some people go through their entire career without telling anyone that they have a diagnosis, others tell every single employer they ever have. In the end the decision is up to you.

Question:

I am terrified of making mistakes at work. What do I do if I make one?

Advice and Guidance:

A lot of people are afraid to make a mistake, particularly in the workplace, but mistakes are part of life. Every single person in the world makes them at some point. You can worry and avoid doing things in case you are a mistake but that can be very limiting and result in you not being fulfilled or trying things you would actually be good at. Mistakes can actually be a great opportunity to learn. You can look at the mistake and reflect on what went wrong and how you are addressing this now and will address it in the future.

Mistakes at work can be challenging particularly when you haven't been working in your role for very long, some tips about making mistakes at work include:

- Remember it isn't the end of the world. If nobody was killed or injured as a result of your mistake and the company your work for hasn't lost millions of dollars due to your mistake it is probably more of an inconvenience than a disaster and is OK.

- As soon as you discover the mistake tell your supervisor. Trying to hide mistakes almost always escalates the consequences on you. Even though your manager might be upset by the mistake, you telling them about it early on is a great demonstration of your ethics and professionalism. Conversely hiding it in the hope they won't find out will probably make you look underhanded and unprofessional.

- Don't try to blame someone else for your mistake.

- Try not to 'beat yourself up' over the mistake worrying and stressing. It is likely that nobody else is anywhere near as bothered by it as you are.

- Try to learn from the mistake and use your understanding of what happened to help you to improve your performance in the future.

- If the mistake does have serious consequences, try to take one day at a time and not fear the worst. This is difficult to do. It can help to have somebody to talk about issues with and offer reassurance.

WHAT DO AUTISTIC YOUNG WOMEN NEED TO KNOW TO EQUIP THEM TO LEAVE HOME?

Question:

Should autistic young women stay at home for longer than their non-autistic sisters?

Advice and Guidance:

As with all people, each autistic young woman is different from the next, as are their non-autistic siblings. As a rule of thumb, it might be better for autistic young women to stay at home longer to enable them to build their confidence and understanding of the world. However, some autistic women are more resourceful, confident and knowledgeable about life than their non-autistic peers as always. use your judgement and see each autistic individual as just that, an individual. For some autistic women, the desire to move out of their childhood home is a huge motivator to develop skills and independence and for these young women, staying in the parental home longer than 17 or 18 is demoralizing.

For parents it is wise to avoid absolutes, such as saying 'You will move out of home at 19' or even 'the best time to move out of home is 19'. This can have a perverse consequence of your daughter forcing herself to move out by 19 even if she is nowhere near ready. It is preferable to have a set of thresholds of knowledge, skills and experience as the point to determine whether your daughter should move out now or later. In this instance, demonstrating flexibility and an ability to adjust the decision about when to move out according to readiness is usually a good idea.

Some teens are desperate to leave home when there is little or no indication that they will manage independent living. Other autistic young women say that they will not leave home under any circumstances. Usually neither of these approaches by teens is being intentionally difficult. Interestingly, often a teen starts off saying that they will never leave home and then as they start to develop more skills, they start talking about wanting to leave home.

Supported living arrangements are still 'leaving home' and can be set up positively by talking about them as shared houses or flatting arrangements and discussing and visiting various options over the years. Around the world funding arrangements for autistics with very high support needs are changing and the possibility of fully personalized supported living exists in some countries. In this case, these types of living arrangements should be explored when the autistic individual is wanting and needing to have more adult choices, and preferably prior to the time when parents cannot manage any longer due to aging.

I (Jeanette) moved out of home when I was 17 and people told me how young I was to move out of home. I responded by saying I had never been any older and didn't know I was young. And I honestly didn't. I knew how to pay rent, cook, work and use public transport but I wasn't very emotionally intelligent at that time. This meant I was able to do most of the practical elements of living independently but was emotionally immature and consequently very lonely as I wanted friends and had very few. And while I wanted friendship in fact I more frequently came to the attention of predatory men rather than kind friends and had no understanding of how to stay safe.

Whereas, I (Emma) left school and moved into my partner's home age 18. When I look back, I can see how much of my masking and acting skills I was using to 'play house' but I do not regret it and it helped me to grow and develop skills that I needed to manage life as an adult. However, I had been to boarding school for many years prior and was very pragmatic and like Jeanette, had many practical skills.

Question:

When it is the right time to leave home?

Advice and Guidance:

In much the same way as it does for non-autistic young people, the right age to move out for autistic women is not set in stone. There is not a number although generally leaving home before the typical high school leaving age of 18 or thereabouts often generates some additional challenges. If your daughter is able to manage practical things she is more likely to succeed at living independently. These practical things include using public transport and/or driving, managing a personal budget, being able to work and/or manage accessing and maintaining appropriate and necessary welfare payments, understanding the need for, and how to ensure, their personal safety, have effective communication, whether speech or alternative communication, to ensure needs are met and knowing how to cook, clean and take care of themselves in terms of hygiene.

One thing to remember is that non-autistic young people can struggle with moving out of home too. This is likely to be a stressful time for you and your daughter, but that is to be expected to an extent, as leaving home is one of the biggest transitions a person will experience, and transitions are challenging. It doesn't matter what age this transition happens, whether 17 or 37, there will still be challenges and excitement. Waiting until 'the right time' will not prevent this and can exacerbate difficulties if there are interpersonal difficulties in the family home.

Question:

How will I know that my daughter will be able to or is ready to leave home?

Advice and Guidance:

Parents usually knew their children better than anyone except the child themselves. The 'gut instincts' a parent has about big decisions their child takes are usually quite accurate. Quite often when something concerns a parent but which their teen or young adult is unconcerned about, it turns out to be the parent's concern which is validated. Teenagers and young adults, autistic and neurotypical alike, have less life experience than their parents and often do not see the potential for difficulties or challenges that their parents probably would.

A respectful and reciprocal relationship with your autistic daughter is a great thing to have or cultivate if you do not have it already. Teenage rebellion can often be viewed as testing both parental and societal boundaries by the teen. They may well want to see those boundaries put in place by a prenatal 'no!'. It is important to set boundaries with your kids and especially teenagers and young adults. If you have a good relationship with your teen daughter which is reciprocal and respectful it can make it a lot easier to manage discussions around moving out of home and knowing when it is right for her to move out. In addition, the way that you parent at this time is role modelling parenting for your autistic daughter. I (Emma) know that I used many of the same parenting techniques as my mother.

When you have a good/positive relationship with your autistic teen you can discuss and/or evaluate their life skills more accurately and let them know why it is helpful to learn any missing skills at home before moving out. Nearly all young adult autistics will be able to leave home, whether it is to move into a sleep out at the bottom of the garden, fully supported accommodation or independent living.

Question:

What skills do autistic spectrum young women need to have to ensure their transition from home to independent living is successful?

Advice and Guidance:

The table below lists many of the skills needed for successful independent living and puts them into categories of the sorts of skills needed to do them. This is not an exhaustive list. A young woman does not need every single one of these skills in order to move out, however the more life skills she has, the fewer challenges she will face following her move.

Life skill	Area it relates to
► Understanding the main unwritten rules of share house living ('don't eat housemate's food without asking, don't walk into their room without knocking and asking if it's OK to come in etc)	Living with housemates
► Abel to respectfully assert needs where required	
► Understanding and respecting reasonable rules of the house	
► Knowing who is responsible for paying for rent, bills, food, maintenance etc	
► Being able to respect and set boundaries with housemates	

Life skill	Area it relates to
▸ Use recipes - written or video ▸ Cook food (from scratch or reheating store bought) ▸ Food safety and food handling ▸ Shopping for food ▸ Eating healthily	Cooking
▸ Managing garbage collections - putting out bins etc ▸ Understanding the process of getting repairs done while renting ▸ Reporting damage or faults to real estate agent / property owner (or if owning, fixing or organising repairs) ▸ Gardening ▸ Minor jobs around the house - e.g. Change light bulbs	Home maintenance

Life skill	Area it relates to
▶ At home or laundromat: ▶ Using the machine ▶ Ensuring clothes are washed ▶ Drying, folding / ironing and putting away clothes	Doing laundry
▶ Tidying ▶ Dusting ▶ Vacuuming ▶ Washing, drying and putting away dishes ▶ Managing clutter: knowing what and when to throw things out	Cleaning house
▶ Going to shops / online shopping ▶ Managing money and budgeting ▶ Buying mostly healthy foods ▶ Making shopping lists - organisational skills	Shopping

Life skill	Area it relates to
▶ Paying enough rent on time ▶ Cleaning for home inspections ▶ Responding to inspection reports ▶ Ensuring home is looked after ▶ Keeping home secure - locking doors, managing keys etc ▶ Reporting issues ▶ Knowing rights as a tenant	Renting property

Life skill	Area it relates to
▸ Understanding the concept of consent in sexual activity	Personal safety
▸ Understanding that the only person who gets to decide what to do with your body is you	
▸ Have some strategies to use in risky situations	
▸ Have an understanding of some of the warning signs of predatory behaviour (such as man buying you lots of alcoholic drinks or giving you drugs)	
▸ Knowing what to do when you are in danger from predators	

Question:

My daughter is 28 and has not taken steps to move out and says she wants to live with us forever. I think she is capable of living out of home, possibly without a lot of assistance. What should I do?

Advice and Guidance:

In recent years in many countries there has been a tendency for young people to live at home for much longer periods than their parents did before them. For autistic young people this can be exacerbated due to difficulties completing education courses or finding and retaining employment. Some autistic people will pick up on the views of those who focus only on their apparent deficits and what they can't do rather than looking at their strengths. Many autistic women lack confidence and are anxious about change, even those changes which are largely positive. These factors can all contribute to an autistic young woman not wanting to leave home.

Some strategies can be put in place which help build independent living skills. These include finding suitable employment or voluntary work, involvement in activities related to their interest or passion and a social group of supportive friends, who might be autistic or neurodivergent themselves. All these things can boost the confidence of the young woman. The skills required for moving out of home often involve good self-confidence and self-esteem and a level of resilience. Building resilience is likely to be an excellent strategy for a young woman not wanting to leave home.

Strategies to acquire resilience often revolve around a person being given the opportunity to work through a set of controlled challenges, in this case focused on the goal of moving out of home. Ideally most of the challenges will be achieved and through each of these the young woman's level of self-confidence and mastery will increase. This is often not a short-term solution and can take months or years to build someone's resilience to the point they are able to leave home. There is a great positive knock-on effect of building resilience around leaving home, as the challenges to build resilience around leaving home will almost certainly translate across other areas of the young woman's life and enable her to approach other changes more confidently in the future.

It will also be useful to find out why she doesn't want to move out and to reassure her that you will still love her and still be involved in her life. If she has fears, address those before pushing her to move out. If someone is made to leave home, they are less likely to be successful than if they choose to move out. If she will need supported accommodation, meet with a variety of providers WITH your daughter to gauge which one is most likely to suit her and meet her needs best.

Question:

My daughter left home after we had a huge argument. We hardly hear from her, even 12 months later. I am really frightened for her welfare. What can I do to show her support without crowding her and help her know we love and support her?

Advice and Guidance:

This is a difficult situation. While it may seem quite negative and frightening, the fact that your daughter is still in contact even infrequently is a very good thing. While each young person is different, in this kind of situation a good course of action often involves letting the young person know they are supported and accepted by their parents and that should they wish to access help they will be able to. While it is incredibly stressful for parents to not know what is going on and to want to intervene by insisting their daughter come home right away this may have the perverse consequence of alienating the young woman and meaning there is even less contact with family.

Hard though it may be, remind yourself that time

changes people and situations and offer support until hopefully your daughter seeks closer contact with you. The exception to this is if your daughter is in imminent danger from sexual predators or criminals or is acutely / frequently suicidal or is engaging in activities which put her in significant danger. In such instances the seriousness of the situation and potential for death or danger outweighs the need to keep your daughter onside in the hope she will be friendly with you again.

If your daughter is at imminent danger from others who are carrying out criminal acts, you should report this to the police, being explicit about your concerns and the exact vulnerabilities that your daughter has, whether due to her autism or something else. If your daughter is actively suicidal you can seek support of the local mental health crisis team, or alternatively take her for a mental health assessment if she will agree. In many countries you can take steps to have someone 'sectioned under the mental health act' which means that they are admitted to a psychiatric hospital against their will for treatment. This is a very serious step and will often result in your daughter refusing to talk to you for some time. However, if this will save her life then it is a useful and important step to take. Someone needs to be significantly unwell due to mental illness for this to happen.

Sending an email or text or even a letter periodically to say hello, that you are thinking about them and hope things are going well can be a good starting point. You could also offer practical support every now and then, for example paying for their mobile phone or sending a care package of food.

Question:

What is involved with renting?

Advice and Guidance:

There are a number of elements involved in renting property. The table below sets out what these are and what someone renting needs to do to ensure they adhere to expectations and rules:

Here are the elements of renting and what the renter has to do.

Who do you deal with when renting?

A rental property is owned by someone who is usually referred to as the owner or landlord. Rental agreements for many properties are managed by a real estate agency. You need to find out who you will be dealing with when you start renting as this determines who you pay the rent to, who does inspections and so forth.

You have rights and responsibilities as a tenant. Find out what these are. Make sure you adhere to your end of the agreement. If the property owner or real estate agent breaches the rules find out where you can go to seek redress.

Paying rent

The amount and frequency of rent payments varies and is set by the owner of the property and detailed in the rental contract.

You need to pay the whole amount of the rent by the due date.

If for whatever reason you are unable to pay the full amount of rent, it is better to discuss this with the owner or the real estate agency managing your rental, preferably prior to the due date. As soon as you have the rent money, pay what is owning to the owner of real estate agency.

If you do not pay rent on several occasions you can be evicted.

As a portion of your budget, rent and food need to be the top priorities, followed by power and water if you are responsible for these.

Bond/security deposit

When you enter into a rental agreement you will need to pay a bond which is also known as a security deposit. You may also be required to pay one month's rent in advance before you move in. These are usual expectations in rental agreements. The point of this is to ensure that if the tenants damage the property or leave a mess which requires a professional cleaner or if they do not pay rent and are evicted that the owner is covered financially. It is unlikely that any of these things will happen, but it covers the owner in case they do.

The bond / security deposit is paid prior to the tenant moving in and refunded when they move out. Sometimes the owner will keep part of the security deposit for outstanding rent payments or damage to the property.

Signing the lease

A rental agreement is a contract. You agree to pay rent and ensure the property is all looked after, and the owner agrees to allow you to live in the property for a specified period or on an ongoing basis, the owner is responsible for some types of necessary repairs. The contract for a rental agreement is called a lease.

When you start a tenancy, you will be required to sign the lease. If you are sharing the property with others it is sensible to ensure they also sign the lease.

Otherwise if they don't pay their rent or damage the property and you are the only person who has signed the lease then you will be legally responsible for any action taken by the property owner.

Read over the lease document and see if there is anything you don't understand, or which looks like it needs to be clarified before you sign. It can help to have someone with experience in these things, for example a parent or even a lawyer, have a look too, just to make sure.

If you are in a shared house arrangement be careful about going or not going on the lease. Being a signatory to the lease means you take financial responsibility for housemates damage to the property. This means you may not be able to get your security deposit back even if you weren't the person causing the damage.

Inspections

During a tenancy the owner or real estate agency will book in regular property inspections. These are usually every three to six months.

The inspection is a time when the owner or agent can check whether you are looking after the property. It involves them checking in each room and in the garden (if there is one). Inspections can be quite stressful, but they are a normal part of renting.

The best thing to do in preparation for an inspection is to clean the property as thoroughly as you can. Make sure there are no dirty dishes, dust and vacuum the whole property, clean the windows if you can get to them, dust away any spiderwebs and clean the bathroom and kitchen thoroughly. If you live in a shared house, then make sure your housemates and/or partner are cleaning as well!

If there is a garden you will need to keep that as healthy as possible. This includes watering regularly to ensure plants don't die and weeding. If there are restrictions on water usage where you live, then it may be helpful to seek advice from the owner or real estate agent as to what their wishes are with watering the garden to ensure compliance with restrictions.

After the inspection the owner or agent will provide you with a report. This will include any jobs you need to do in order to ensure the property is well maintained. You will need to address anything raised in the inspection report.

Who is responsible for maintenance?

Maintenance of the property such as plumbing, electrical and the structure of the house is the responsibility of the owner.

If you are able to change a light bulb, unblock drains or fix a washer on tap that is OK but anything beyond that needs to be reported to the property owner as soon as possible after you identify an issue. The property owner is responsible for paying for this maintenance. You are responsible for the furniture and other non-structural things.

Can I have pets if I am renting?

The answer to this is yes. And no. Basically whether or not to allow pets in a rental property comes down to individual property owners. Some will be happy for you to have a pet and others won't allow pets.

It is important to ask about pets before you move in either if you already have a pet or if you plan to get one. There is often a clause about pet ownership not being allowed in lease agreements.

If you have an assistance animal then, in some countries, a property owner has to allow you to keep your assistance animal with you by law. However, some people who have assistance animals tell stories about property owners discriminating against them and not understanding or following the law. So once again, if you have an assistance animal or you want to bring an animal into the home with you then it is a good idea to discuss that prior to signing your lease.

Please note that social/state housing (provided by the government/state) rental is slightly different. For example, the lease is usually for life or linked to income status and there are no regular inspections. Supported accommodation is also slightly different, with each provider managing this differently.

PRACTICAL LIFE SKILLS FOR AUTISTIC YOUNG WOMEN

Question:

I have a job, but I don't earn a lot of money. How can I budget effectively?

Advice and Guidance:

Making a personal budget is an essential part of living independently. Having a budget allows you to get the most out of your money and ensure you don't run out. It is good to be able to save money for things you want to do but more important to ensure all your basic living costs are covered; rent/mortgage, food, bills, travel to and from work.

Try and keep a little money over each pay period, this could be each week, fortnight, or even month. Allocate a small amount to keep, and save it in a separate bank account, as you don't know when a large bill might come in or you might unexpectedly need to go to the doctor or pay for specialist treatment. It can be helpful to open separate bank accounts for different things, like a savings account, an account for car loan payments and an account for regular expenses like food and rent. However, if the bank charges you for each account, you may prefer to have one account and track everything in detail online.

Your budget will need to change when your financial circumstances change. For example, if you were employed before but are currently unemployed you will need to adjust your budget accordingly. It can be helpful to use a document or a budgeting app to record your budget and spending. Some apps can calculate all the different elements of your budget.

The sorts of things you include in your budget will be specific to you but there are some things which most people include. These are:

- Rent / mortgage / board
- Food – learning to cook can save you money if you make your own meals from real ingredients
- Transport - car / public transport / taxis / Uber - you can save money by walking or cycling
- Bills - phone / internet / electricity / gas / water – you can save money by going with the cheapest provider and often get a discount if you pay on time
- Entertaining – going out / games and apps / restaurants and pubs – this is the one that should be stopped if your income decreases
- Savings

If you live at home with your family or carers, the best thing you can do with your money is to save as much as you can. it's better to keep your money for a time for when you may need it, for example when you move out of home. Saving a rental security deposit or deposit for a mortgage is a good place to start.

Here is an example of a fairly basic budget:

Example Budget

Salary (monthly): $1080 (after tax)

Expenses per month:
Rent - $ 400
Food - $120
Transport (bus) - $30
Transport (taxi/uber) - $60
Medication - $21 ($42 per month)
Bills - electricity, gas and water - $80
Bills - phone and Internet - $85
Savings - $125
Entertaining - $120

Subtotal - $1042

This leaves $38 after all expenses are paid.

Question:

How do I know if I should go for my driver's licence? I want to drive but I'm anxious and people have told me I would be a terrible driver?

Advice and Guidance:

Many people, whether or not they are on the autism spectrum, initially struggle with learning to drive. Very few people are good drivers without lots of practice. My mother always told me to assume that every driver is a bad driver, this advice has made me a cautious driver. Unless you have additional disabilities that make it impossible for you to drive, you ought to be able to learn to drive. Adapted cars are available in some countries for people with additional disabilities to learn to drive in and then to drive.

Learning to drive can be very anxiety provoking, but this is the case for most people, not just you! In general, if you have a good reason to get a driving license, you will be more motivated to work hard at learning the skills needed. I failed my first driving test and then passed the second time.

Question:

What is involved in getting a driver's license?

Advice and Guidance:

Every state/territory/country has their own regulations around getting a driver's license. In many places the first step is to get a learner's license or permit. This usually means that you can only drive when a full license holder is also in the car and the car has L plates (stickers) displayed clearly. Some places you need to do a test to get this license and others you do not.

Next you need to learn to drive! In some places, it is mandated/required that you do a certain number of lessons with a registered driving instructor, whilst in others you can learn with any adult with a full license. Most people find it easier to learn from a professional driving instructor as you can ask the driving school to provide someone with particular characteristics. For example, I asked for someone with lots of patience, who would never shout at me. I would regularly stall the car when I was first learning and my first instructor would shout at me, telling me what to do, but the shouting was overwhelming and instead of complying, I would panic. Once I had got a more patient instructor, I learnt much more quickly.

You then have to sit a practical test (and often a written/oral or computerized test on the road rules). The examiner sits in the car with you and gives you instructions for the duration of the driving test. They assume you know the road rules and will not provide guidance on those. As an example, the instructor might ask you to take the next road on the left, if you turn left but forget to indicate or stop first at a stop sign, you have broken the road rules. If you break the road rules or drive badly, you usually fail the test. You can usually retake the test as often as you like, though it costs money each time you do!

In some places when you have passed this test you still hold a provisional license for a period of time, and only at the end of that time does it become a full license. During this time there are some restrictions around the house of the day that you can drive, who can be in the car and the amount of alcohol that you can drink and drive. It is always better to not drink or take recreational drugs before driving as they impair your reaction time and can make it more likely that you will crash.

Question:

I just got my license and want to buy a car. Where do I start? And what should I be aware of as I hear some people selling cars are not trustworthy?

Advice and Guidance:

The first car I bought cost me $100 and was 'a heap of

junk', the engine caught fire on my way to work and I had to give it to the scrap metal merchants to tow it away from my workplace! After this I learnt to only buy a car that had been first checked by a mechanic I trust and/or still has some warranty on it. This is difficult if you have a low income, but I am an obsessive saver and so used my savings to buy my second car. Over the years, I have had good cars and cars that fell apart when driven on the freeway.... Once I earned enough to buy a new car, I bought a car with a 5 year warranty which meant that when things went wrong they got fixed without me needing to pay for them. Car repairs are VERY expensive, and this often results in people needing to pay more for repairs than the car is worth on cheap cars.

Always take someone with you when you go and look at a car for sale (for safety) and ask to take it for a test drive as you may not like the way some cars feel to drive. Make sure the car is powerful enough to drive up a hill if you need it to be!

Question:

I have a driver's licence, but I just moved to a big city and I can't drive in the middle of town, so I need to take public transport. I have never done it before and am very anxious. What are some strategies to help me to feel OK and be safe on public transport?

Advice and Guidance:

A lot of autistic people are anxious about public transport. Many non-autistic people also get concerned about their physical safety on public transport, but autistic people can have additional concerns. Potential issues include being worried they will miss their stop, strangers talking to them, discrimination, people misunderstanding their motives and behaviour and the transport itself arriving late or early, either due to practical concerns around punctuality or sensitivity about transport arriving late or early.

There are a few strategies which are likely to make using public transport less stressful. These include:

- Having a physical or online timetable with you when you are using the bus. You may prefer to use the transport company's app, which will usually plan your route for you and step out what you need to do. Some of the apps even have maps of where you need to walk, and the route taken by the bus/tram/train. Some apps also alert you to when you need to get off the tram/train/bus, whilst others just tell you what bus/tram/train stop you need and it is up to you to recognize it.

- Practice using public transport when it is likely that not very many people will be using it. This will usually be between about 10-2:30 on weekdays or early morning (before 9am) on weekends. You can also ask a friend or family member to come with you a couple of times too, this can help you build your confidence.

- There can sometimes be special events which impact the number of people using public transport, so you can go to get the bus thinking it will be quiet and then find out that there are 1000 football fans going to a match! It can help to be aware of upcoming events and avoid using public transport when a major event is taking place if possible.

- Listen to music and/or wear noise-cancelling headphones. This can alleviate stress and also usually means other people are less likely to try to engage you in conversation. It is perfectly socially acceptable to wear headphones on public transport, although it is important not to play your music so loudly that other people can hear it too!

- If you are concerned about getting off at the wrong

stop there are a few strategies. You can count stops between your stop and where you are going. You can also find a landmark you recognise as being at your stop or the stop before. If it is dark or raining heavily it can help to sit next to the window so you can be sure to see the stops or landmark. On a bus, when you get on, you can ask the driver to tell you when it is your stop. Some trams and trains have conductors or guards and they may also tell you. However, do not rely on this alone as they can forget, and I have had this happen to me a number of times, so now I rely on transport apps.

▸ Some people are concerned about personal safety on public transport, particularly on trains or trams where there is no conductor or guard. Trains and trams in many cities now have an intercom which you can press for emergency assistance. This will alert staff or police that there is a problem. If you are concerned, then try to sit near the intercom. There are some times of the day which feel safer to travel, if you are concerned about personal safety. These include during daylight and/or before about 9:00 pm. However, it is sensible to take a self-defence class and learn some skills to help you feel more confident. Some women also carry a rape alarm, where these are legal. If it is legal where you live, and you chose to do this, you need to hold it in your hand all the time or it will be of no use. I used to keep mine in my pocket and hold it in my hand, so no-one could see it.

It is often helpful to develop a set of strategies for using public transport which work for you. Using public transport is often a skill which people grow in confidence with practice. This means that while you might be very anxious when you start using public transport but the more you do it you are likely to build your resilience and confidence around using public transport. Being able to use public transport is a lot cheaper than using taxis or uber and if you do not drive it can give you a considerable amount of independence.

Question:

My daughter chooses to eat four things, none of which are vegetables. While she has been at home we have encouraged her to eat foods beyond her preference which she is OK about. I am concerned now she is leaving home that her eating won't be very healthy. She is already very thin. What can I do to help her eat a varied diet once she leaves home?

Advice and Guidance:

This is very difficult as it depends what the four things are, why she has this preference and her general attitude to and understanding of nutrition and health. If she is able to be healthy on her restricted diet then it is better to just let her be comfortable in her food choices, as leaving home can be quite a stressful period for some people, autistic or not. If however, she is not healthy and is malnourished it may help to ask her if she is willing to come and visit a nutritionist with you to talk about how to make small modifications to her diet to improve her health. For example, if your daughter likes hard beige food, it might be about finding some other beige hard food that has higher nutrients or looking at if she could tolerate taking multivitamins.

Sometimes, when autistics leave home they make lots of large and significant changes, so it is possible that she will become more adventurous in her food choices and preferences. However, there are a number of people, both autistic and not who eat just a small number of food items throughout their lives.

Question:

What do I need to know about healthcare now that I've moved out of home?

Advice and Guidance:

Your physical and mental health, including dental health, are the most important assets you have. Poor physical or mental health make it difficult or impossible to take part in all the other elements of life like education, employment, recreation and relationships. When you live at home with family / carers they will usually look out for your health, for example by arranging regular dental and GP check-ups, taking you to the emergency department if you need to go and reminding you to take medications or other treatments for health issues. When you move out of home, this becomes your own responsibility. It is helpful to consider that taking care of your health has a number of elements. These elements of health care include:

- Managing ongoing health conditions
    - Taking medication as prescribed
    - Renewing prescriptions for regular medication you take
    - Making and attending appointments with doctors to maintain your health if you have an ongoing health condition.
- Seeking treatment for any new illnesses or health conditions
    - Knowing when to seek help and who to seek help from
    - Sexual health checks
    - Dental health checks
    - Eating healthily - a balanced diet of veg-

etables and fruits, proteins, carbohydrates, dairy (or another source of calcium if you are intolerant or allergic to dairy), and a small amount of sugars and fats.

- ▸ When people move out of home their diet can become less healthy than when they were living at home. This is not a disaster but is not very healthy if it continues long term. It can be helpful to see your diet when you move out as being an anomaly, a 'honeymoon period' which is part of your celebrations for independence or temporary lack of budgeting skills! After a few weeks remind yourself you need to eat healthily so that 'honeymoon period' needs to end and usual health eating recommences.

▸ Exercise is important. Most people in Western counties have difficulty getting enough exercise and obesity is a significant problem. Some people dislike gyms or cannot afford the fees. This is OK. Exercise can involve things like walking / running, swimming or sports. If you have anxiety about going to the gym but enjoy using the equipment you can get gym equipment for your own home. Walking is a free and easy way to exercise if this is possible for you. If not, you can find out if you can access a swimming pool or accessible gym or sports team/activity such as sailability.

▸ Exercise is useful for increasing or maintaining physical strength and fitness, losing weight if you need to and staying physically healthy. Exercise and being physically active are also very important in mental health and can really help with a sense of wellbeing over time.

▸ Activities often become habitual if you do them for around one month. This means that if you practice healthy eating and exercise for a month or more, it is likely to become part of your routine, During that first month you may need to convince yourself to continue the healthy practice and work hard to do it, then it is likely to pay off in the longer term though becoming habitual and 'business as usual' in your life. I have hated exercise for many years but had a six-week membership to an aerial yoga 'gym' and at the end of the six weeks it was a habit and I was starting to feel better and see the physical benefits. I am still going a year later.

Question:

I know that autistics are more likely to experience mental illness, how can I look after my mental health?

Advice and Guidance:

It is important to be aware of your mental health. Things like anxiety, depression and psychosis do occur relatively commonly for autistic people and these can sometimes first appear around the teenage or young adult years. There are protective factors around good mental health.

These include things like:

▸ Valuing and respecting yourself

▸ Having a positive identity as an autistic person

▸ Being engaged in an activity which is meaningful for you, this could be paid work but doesn't need to be. Autistic people usually have a passion or interest. Doing things related to your interest can be incredibly meaningful. Avoiding illicit drugs and excessive alcohol

▸ A sense of belonging, be that with family or people who share your interests or other friends

▸ Being surrounded by people who like and respect

you

If you have an ongoing condition managing your mental health might include things like:

- Making and keeping appointments with your psychiatrist, therapist or psychologist

- If you have moved away recently seeking out a new psychiatrist, psychologist or therapist. This can be challenging, and it is a good idea to discuss with people you trust such as family members or close friends. You can also ask others you know in the area as to which therapist or psychologist they use and might recommend.

- Taking medications as prescribed. It can help to have a dosette pack or ask the pharmacist to make you a pack of your medication which has the days of the week and times to take the different medications. The pharmacist will usually charge a small fee for this service, but it is a very good idea, particularly if you have a number of different medications or you often forget to take your medication.

Question:

How often do I need to see the doctor?

Advice and Guidance:

It is a very good idea to see your general practitioner (GP) at least once a year for a check-up, even if you feel healthy. It is also a good idea to find a GP that you like and who listens to you. If you find a good GP, keep seeing them as your regular GP. A lot of the issues when people change doctors is that there is no continuity of their medical care. A GP you have been seeing for years will probably have a much better understanding of you and your health than one you see for the first time.

Autistic people often struggle with something called interoception. Interoception is the awareness of what is going on in the body. Atypical or inaccurate interoception can have serious implications for medical care. Firstly, it means we may not realize we need to access healthcare and may be very sick before we know that something is wrong. It can also make conversations with medical professionals very difficult as we can struggle to explain what is happening and be understood. If you have difficulties with interoception including not noticing physical health difficulties, then it is a good idea to make an appointment with the doctor as soon as you are aware something feels not quite right. It is far preferable to have a false alarm than miss a serious medical problem.

In terms of talking with your doctor about your physical health issues, it can help to go to the appointment with a written list of symptoms you are aware of and any Questions you want to ask them. If you are concerned about not being listened to you can take an advocate or support person in with you, this can be a close friend, parent, partner, support worker (if you have one) or sibling. You can write down what the doctor says as well, especially if they prescribe medication or other treatments and give instructions about the treatment. It is also ok to ask the doctor to write down what they are telling you so that you can process it afterwards.

If you take regular medication you will need to see your doctor frequently to ensure the medication is and continues to be effective and that you are not experiencing any problematic side effects or complications.

Even if you feel fine, you should see your GP for a

check-up at least every twelve months regardless of age and fitness level and you should see your GP if you feel unwell in addition to the symptoms of any conditions you already have diagnosed and treated.

Question:

How do I know if a medical complaint is serious and needs urgent treatment and when it can wait? I am not good at identifying sensations in my body so this is always challenging. Are there strategies which might help?

Advice and Guidance:

This can be a real issue for many autistic people. Many autistics, due to atypical interoception, do not notice physical pain or other symptoms until they are severe. Others, again due to atypical interoception, are so sensitive and aware of pain that people see them as being hypochondriacs and therefore dismiss any symptoms they complain of. Both scenarios can be very dangerous and result in death or serious illness and injury, if treatment is not provided or even requested.

It often helps to enlist the support of a close friend, family members or your partner if you have one to assist you in noticing symptoms and health concerns. You can talk about your symptoms or medical concerns to your support person. They may be able to see your pain or other symptoms more objectively. They may also know when something you are experiencing is concerning where you might not be too worried. For many autistics who do not 'feel' their pain or illness, their behaviour changes when they are unwell, or their sensory preferences change in some significant way. Other people may notice these more quickly than you do, and it is at this point you should seek a medical evaluation from a GP or if you or others are seriously concerned you can go to an emergency department.

You can also talk to your GP and ask them to give you a list of some symptoms which are red flags for serious illness or injury. You can start to observe your health experiences. If you have missed something in the past but have learned what the warning signs were so you can seek help quicker in the future if that issue occurs again. You can improve your sense of interoception to help you assess whether an injury is minor (requiring no assistance), medium, (requiring first aid) or major (requiring immediate medical treatment), through becoming more aware of your body. To do this you can change something about your body and focus on what that feels like. For example, having a relaxed hand and then stretching the fingers as wide apart as possible and really focusing on what that feels like and where you can feel it. Doing this several times a day for a few minutes, with various parts of your body, really does help you to connect to your body and develop more accurate interoception.

It is not a good idea to search out symptoms and health conditions on the internet unless you are a medical professional yourself or have an excellent knowledge of human anatomy and disease. Internet medical sites vary in quality and many of them will come up with only the most serious medical conditions which could be caused by your symptoms. Because autistic people can struggle to pinpoint what is going on in their body, here sites can be counterproductive and make you think you have cancer when you just have a cold, for example.

One strategy you can use if you are unsure as to whether or not to seek medical assistance, is a nurse on call service which exists in some countries. This free service (apart from the cost of the phone call) usually involves calling a phone number and speaking with a registered nurse or nurse practitioner. You explain to them the symptoms which are concerning you and they provide what they consider the most appropriate course of action. However, it should be noted that the nurses have a duty of care to ensure you don't ignore a serious issue. This means that they tend to be very risk averse and recommend you see a doctor urgently for anything they can't immediately diagnose. Coupled with the difficulty many autistic people have in articulating and noticing health issues, this service is not useful for everyone.

Question:

I have depression which I take medication for. What sorts of mental health services are available? How do I get help if I need it urgently?

Advice and Guidance:

A mental health condition like depression needs to be managed. This usually includes a number of different strategies such as working on psychology and thinking styles, taking medication, looking after your physical health and ensuring you have support and have meaning in your life, in whatever form that may take.

Living independently can be challenging if you have depression but it is certainly not an unattainable goal. It may mean you move out of home in a mode incremental way and spend time at the family home and in your new home to see how well you are managing the move to independent living.

Living independently can mean you see less of people who care about you or know you well. This can cause difficulties for people who have a mental health condition. One of the useful things about living at home with family or carers is that they are more likely to notice when you are having a hard time.

Given that many autistic people have alexithymia or emotion blindness and/or poor interoception, they may struggle to recognize when they are getting un-well with depression. If this is an issue for you, it is important to keep in regular contact with people that know and care about you. If you are geographically distant than book in a regular chat on Skype (or a similar video chat) so they can see how you are doing and alert you if they are concerned about your mood or wellbeing.

Question:

Is it possible for an autistic woman to buy property?

Advice and Guidance:

Many people, including autistic people, buy and sell property. However, there are a lot of things you need to know about buying property. It can be quite a daunting prospect if you haven't done so before, or even if you have! Buying a home is probably the big-gest purchase you will ever make. Most people have to borrow a lot of money to fund their purchase. A mort-gage can take decades to pay off, with lending usually planned to be repaid over 25–30 years.

These are the steps needed to buy a home sequential-ly:

1. The first step in buying a home is to work out if you have enough money, which consists of two parts – a deposit of up to 20% of the price of a property and proof of enough income to meet the repayments. You can make an appointment with a bank loans officer or

with a mortgage broker who will calculate how much money they will lend you for a mortgage based on your income and savings and any loans or debts that you have. Note: Banks and lenders may offer you a larger amount than you can reasonably afford if interest rates increase. If you borrowed that amount you could make the repayments from your income but probably couldn't do much else! Being cautious in financial decisions is a very good idea. One useful resource is the mortgage calculators provided on bank websites. You can enter in a number of variables to find out what your mortgage repayments would be on different loan amounts.

2. House hunting: Once you know how much money you can borrow then it is time to look around for homes which suit your needs within your budget. There are websites in different localities which list properties for sale. These are often good places to start. It is usually a good idea to look at a number of properties before committing to one to get an idea about what is out there in your price range. However, sometimes people find the 'perfect' home after looking at very few other properties. Generally, it is wise to get a more thorough idea of the homes which are available in your area and then make a choice. You may decide on a type of housing first, for example a tiny house, an apartment/flat/unit or a house. Note: House prices and interest rates change frequently.

3. Making an offer: When you find the home you really want, contact the real estate agent /realtor who is selling it and make an offer of how much you want to pay. This often involves some negotiation, so a rule of thumb would be to offer a little less on the property than you want to pay along with the conditions of mortgage approval and a satisfactory buildings inspection (and any other conditions your lawyer suggests). If your offer is accepted it is a sort of provisional approval for you to buy the home but there are other steps. You will need to negotiate a settlement

period. This is the time between when you make an offer for the property and when you get the keys!

Auctions: Some houses are sold by auction. This means all the people who want to buy the home make bids in an auction. The highest bidder gets to buy the house. Auctions tend to not be a very autism-friendly kind of sales method, as they are very high stress environments. However, the biggest drawback is that you cannot make conditions on your offer and need to pay within a very short time, if you win the bidding.

4. Once your offer has been accepted it is a very good idea to have a building inspection done on the home to ensure there are not any major maintenance issues. At this point in the process you are not obligated to buy the home if it was a condition of your offer, in which case, if an inspection does turn up any issues you are perfectly at liberty to withdraw your offer.

5, When you are satisfied that you wish to buy the home then you need to engage a lawyer. There are specialist property law firms who specialise in domestic real estate transactions. The lawyer will draw up the contract for the property and have the person selling you the property sign the contract and have you sign the contract. These are then exchanged so each person has a signed copy of the contract. Arrange house insurance (contents and buildings) to start on settlement day.

6. At this point, if you haven't done so already, pack your things and book a moving truck (or ask friends and family to help you move). The next step in the process is the final legal requirement - settlement. You don't have to attend the settlement but some people choose to as buying property can be quite exciting. Once settlement is complete you will receive the keys and you can move in.

7. Move in and congratulate yourself on navigating

the world of real estate sales and having your new home.

HEALTHY ADULT FRIENDSHIPS

Question:

What constitutes a 'friend'?

Advice and Guidance:

Friendship is a concept which is defined by the people in the friendship rather than there being a fixed definition of what constitutes a friend. There are many kinds of friendships, some of which are helpful and others which are not. There are many misconceptions about autistic people and friendship, such as that we do not want friends, are unable to maintain a friendship, that we are naive and gullible friends and that we are all shy introverts who find social contact very difficult and unpleasant. In fact, autistic people have a wide range of social expressions. Non-autistic people who are friends with autistic women, and autistics in general, often remark on what loyal and thoughtful friends we are.

Most people would consider somebody who they enjoy spending time with whether in person, online or by phone, a friend. A friend could be defined as a person who cares for and likes you, somebody you seek advice from and give advice to, someone who regularly visits or messages you and somebody you can trust to look out for your interests. A friend can be a person with or without shared interests to you. Autistic people often have friends who are autistic and / or neurodivergent. A friend is often a person you feel you can go to for advice or to vent about a difficult situation. There is no one kind of friendship - we are all different and our social needs and outlets are different too.

An important concept when thinking about friendships is the idea of 'give and take,' or reciprocity. A good friendship is where each friend does some 'giving' in the friendship and some 'taking.' This is not a static thing and over the course of the friendship the levels of giving and taking will most likely fluctuate. If you have concerns about a friendship it can help to think about instances of giving and taking by you and your friend. If there is a clear imbalance in the giving and taking it is an opportunity to consider any steps you can take to address this.

Just because someone interacts with you, does not mean that they are your friend. Sometimes autistics can misread politeness or professionalism as an indicator of friendship. Your support worker or the person who serves you at the grocery store are not your friend, they are being polite and/or professional. You can make friends with people at work or who work in your local community over time, but they need to want to be friends too.

Online friends are just as valid and valuable for many autistics as those with whom you interact with face to face. For very shy or anxious women, the online world can be easy to be in and an easier place to find and make friends. However, you do need to be aware that online, not everyone is honest about who they are or what they want. To avoid being 'catfished' or duped into a long term online relationship by someone who is pretending to be someone else, ensure that you view everyone with a healthy dose of scepticism. Key indicators someone is a catfish is that they ask for money or other gifts/loans, that they are unable to video chat for various reasons and that they make arrangements to meet you which always fall through, or they refuse to meet you.

Question:

What can go wrong in friendships?

Advice and Guidance:

Friends usually have mostly positive attributes, but friendships can become difficult or toxic. Often this is not simply because one person behaves poorly. It can be the result of a wide range of events and issues which serve to place stress on the friendship. In some cases, this can be remedied and the damage to the friendship repaired. In other instances, it will mean the end of the friendship, not necessarily because either person did anything 'wrong', but just because the friendship couldn't stand up to the challenges.

In some instances, someone you think of as a friend is in fact just using you. They may be a narcissist or bully, for example. You can tell that they are just using you if they are always wanting things; time, attention, money or favours from you, but are never available for you when you want or need some support or just to hang out. People like this tend to prey on autistics because we are quite often trusting and kind. A toxic friendship does not actually bring any real or lasting benefits for you and at their worst can even be a form of abuse or invalidation. There is more information on dealing with unhealthy or toxic friendships later in this chapter.

These are big picture, general sorts of issues with friendships. Some events can happen which threaten to end the friendship which is more specific.

These include:

- Ongoing disagreements on a topic where neither party backs down
- One or both friends feeling they need to be 'right'
- Issues with intimate partner relationships, from frequent criticism of one or other friends' partner to cheating or infidelity
- Offensive comments, for example about autism, gender identity or cultural background
- Somebody not listening to or respecting the wishes of a friend
- Imbalance in a number of domains (salary, education, intellectual capacity, accomplishments etc) leading to disagreements and one friend feeling superior or inferior to the other as a result of this
- Disagreements about parenting style when one or both friends are parents
- One friend became unwell with physical or mental illness. This can lead to a range of challenges such as holding onto comments said or actions done when a friend was unwell, expectations from both parties about caring responsibilities. Feeling that the friendship has become one-sided instead of giving and taking
- Arguments, insults or physical aggression
- Ableism - things like paternalism and 'ablesplaining'
- Misunderstandings
- Frequent disagreements and assumptions made about different values, such as politics or faith

Some of these issues might end a friendship but they do not need to. If you wish to continue a friendship and some of these issues are present, it can often be discussed and worked through. If you are in the wrong, a genuine and heartfelt apology can make a big difference. If you perceive your friend as being in the wrong, trying to understand what might have caused the problem and accepting their apology and forgiving them can help a lot. An interesting point about forgiveness is that it is usually more beneficial to the person doing the forgiving than the person who wronged them. Forgiving someone enables you to move on and let go rather than carrying a load of blame and anger within you.

Question:

What are some of the differences between autistic and non-autistic friends?

Advice and Guidance:

Probably the most significant difference between autistic and neurotypical people is that each group communicates differently, both in the way they give and receive information and the interpretation of the communication and the world around them. This can impact on friendships, sometimes in positive and sometimes in negative ways.

The expectations of what friendship should be like and how friends should behave often differs between autistic and non-autistic people. Interests which autistic people enjoy may seem meaningless to some non-autistic people and vice versa. This does not mean that friendships are not possible between autistic and non-autistic people, but it is important to know some of the differences in approach and communication which can occur, so that you can try to maximize the positive potential of any friendships.

Autistic people may seek out the following qualities in a friend:

- Someone to share time, experience and stories with
- Loyalty
- Honesty
- Reciprocity
- Mutual respect
- Shared interests
- An expectation that the friendship will be ongoing
- Support
- Fun
- Someone to vent to
- Someone to share deep and meaningful conversations and thoughts with
- Someone to share fandoms with

The interesting thing about this list is that the list for non-autistic people is often very similar. Their interests may be different and the definition of 'deep and meaningful' topics may vary but essentially autistic and non-autistic people often want similar qualities in a friendship. This can be a point of commonality which you can work from with a neurotypical friend, even if outwardly they seem very different to you. Some people may not have or wish to have any non-autistic friends but many of us do. Knowing that even while we are different from our non-autistic friends but in many ways, there are points of commonality being us is often a comforting thought.

One of the best ways of managing a friendship with someone who sees the world very differently to us is sharing experiences, learning from each other about how we each experience the world. Talking about differences and explaining motivations and thinking can mean the difference between a friendship which works well and one which doesn't. It is always ok to ask for clarification, and to realize that we can all accidentally hurt the feelings of people we care about when there are misunderstandings or miscommunication.

In a similar way to which we might appear odd to a non-autistic person, they can also baffle us. Some of the things non-autistic friends can do which are confusing or challenging include:

▸ Inviting you to socialize with a group of other people and not understanding why it is overwhelming for you. Non-autistic people often find socializing gives them an energy and emotional boost.

▸ Making small talk and expecting small talk back from an autistic friend. Non-autistics use small talk as a social nicety, they can find people who do not do so rudely.

▸ Having a fascination with your sexual and romantic life. Sex and relationships are normal topics of conversation between many non-autistic good friends and gossip (sharing information about other people when they are not present) can often involve the topics of sex and relationships. It is ok to not gossip, although non-autistics who do gossip can be quite offended if you say that you do not gossip. Because of this, it can be easier to just not join in the gossiping and over time people will stop trying to involve you in gossip.

▸ Being fascinated by your autism and asking lots of Questions about it. In general, non-autistic people are interested in differences and gain the majority of their information from social media and popular culture. If they are respectful in their Questions, and you are happy to answer, it is fine. However, if they are not respectful, it is ok to refuse to answer Questions and if they continue to ask, perhaps you may decide not to be friends with them any longer.

- ▶ Focusing on things which are meaningless to you, such as shopping, fashion or movies. You may or may not be interested in any of these, but your non-autistic friends may or may not share an interest in your passions. It is ok to find an aspect of someone bewildering, and this does not mean that you cannot be friends.

There are some unwritten rules in friendships which non-autistic people seem to pick up on as if by magic, but autistic people can struggle to be aware of. Discussion of 'deep' topics is not always welcome. However, on some occasions it is OK to do it. As it is a 'rule of thumb' (rather than a rule) it can help to check whether your friend is happy to discuss this topic. It works the other way too, your friend might want to check in with you about topics which you find concerning or upsetting before launching into it. Topics non-autistic people might consider 'deep' include personal salary, mental illness, death, political discussions, discussions around religion and / or philosophy, discussion of abuse or sexual violence or personal soul-searching. The tricky thing is that some neurotypical people will be happy to discuss these things sometimes but not all the time. This is something which each person will approach differently and something which may well settle down as your friendship develops. If you find discussing sex too confronting, you can let your friends know when they start to talk about it, that for you, it is too personal, in the same way that they find some topics too personal.

Some friends will ask for your opinion about something and want an honest answer but sometimes they won't. In these situations, it can help to already discuss ground rules around honesty. You can discuss parameters for when it's best to respond 'brutally honestly' and times where they think that a vaguely positive response is best. However, be aware that social niceties mean that even when a friend says that they want an honest answer, they don't always mean this. As an example, when you tell them something true, that they didn't really want to hear, they may take it out on you by saying that you are a horrible person. They may even refuse to take to you ever again. If this happens, it is important that you realize that you did not do anything wrong and that you are not a horrible person. If you think that this might happen, you may want to check if they really want your advice/opinion or if they just want reassurance about their idea/opinion.

There is an expectation by many non-autistic people that their friends should 'back them up' in an argument with other people. If you don't support their side of the story they may become angry, even if they were in the wrong. This can create a big problem for friends. Once again, it can help to discuss this prior to you being expected to back up your friend. If you cannot lie for someone or take sides with someone in the wrong, you should probably be very honest about this when meeting new people.

Knowing when you are expected, or not expected, to pay for meals or drinks with friends can be very difficult for autistic people. There are gendered expectations around this with men in some cultures being expected to pay for a meal or drinks with a woman, even if the woman is wealthier than the man or if they are not in an intimate relationship. Different friends have their own systems for paying. However, even in an agreed arrangement there can be unexpected changes. It is best to ask about whether or not you should pay, or not pay your share for meals or drinks on each occasion you share a meal or drinks with a friend. It can help if you can work out an arrangement with your friend, so you know who is expected to pay for what in different circumstances. 'Going Dutch' is an expression that means each person pays for what they ate and/or drank. Some friends do this all the time, whilst others take turns to pay for things if they go out somewhere together. Wealthier friends may or may not pay for less wealthy friends to do things. If you cannot afford to do something, it is ok to say that you cannot go because you cannot afford it.

Question:

What are boundaries and how do I avoid being 'walked over' in a friendship?

Advice and Guidance:

Setting, reinforcing and responding to boundaries can be difficult. Personal boundaries are guidelines, rules or limits that a person creates to identify reasonable, safe and permissible ways for other people to behave towards them and how they will respond when someone passes those limits. Any interaction between people needs boundaries and limits.[4] These relate to things defining what is and isn't acceptable, what people are prepared to do and what they are not prepared to do. Autistics might be happiest explaining these parameters and limits to one another and agree on them. However non-autistic communication is often more focused on subtlety, nuance and politeness, and a non-autistic person may not know to explain to you about boundaries in your friendship. For those who are not 'out' about their autism with their friends these situations can be particularly tricky. It can be useful to explain things in terms of your needs and experience which does not necessarily require a discussion of autism. Boundaries can relate to things like up until what time of day a person can phone or

[4] Source: http://www.guidetopsychology.com/boundaries.htm
Accessed 15 January 2018

text a friend. For some people it is ok to phone at 2am whilst for others, you can only ring until 9pm.

There are unwritten rules and assumptions around boundaries and limits within friendships. Some autistic people may inadvertently not notice a boundary or overstep a mark without knowing. Their non-autistic friend might have assumed that the boundary was obvious and so misinterpreted when it was overstepped as intentional and indicative of poor behaviour. This situation can be very anxiety-provoking for autistic people. It is one way that communication differences can be thrown into sharp relief. It is not the 'fault' of the autistic person or their non-autistic friend, but the result of different 'languages' being spoken and some words being lost in translation. There can be a positive result from this kind of situation in that, if both parties are willing to understand that there are key differences in their communication, autistic people and non-autistic people can learn to speak a little more of one another's 'language'.

Autistic people have often had negative experiences with friendships. They may have been bullied, excluded or blamed for things they were unaware of even being an issue. Autistic women often have a very strong need for social acceptance and a sense of belonging. The loss or betrayal of a friendship can be traumatic and cause extreme anxiety. This can impact in a few ways, including making us seem needy or clingy as friends or being hyper-vigilant about being good friends. When friendship ends it can cause self-criticism and overthinking. A way of addressing this is to build your self-esteem and self-worth. This is not usually a quick process. It can be supported through a number of practices such as consciously making note of your positive qualities, self-soothing activities and undertaking therapy using a psychological model which is appropriate to you and your needs and experiences. A related issue is where autistic women stay in a friendship that they know to be toxic, abusive or exploitative for fear they may never find another friend and thinking that a toxic friendship is better than being lonely. In fact, a toxic friendship is often a lot worse than being alone because toxic friends eat into your self-esteem and make you doubt yourself. These toxic relationships can make people lonelier than being alone.

Building assertiveness is very useful when thinking about boundaries. Assertiveness is essentially the skill of being able to set limits and enforce boundaries with people, including in friendships. It involves not being passive and simply giving in when someone challenges or attacks your boundary. It also involves not being aggressive and 'shooting down in flames' anyone who doesn't adhere to your boundary or limit. Assertiveness can be a very difficult skill for autistic women who may have low self-esteem or may have difficulty being aware of how their actions might be seen by others.

The key to assertiveness is standing your ground but being respectful. 'I' statements form the basis of assertiveness. This means approaching somebody challenging your boundary using a statement in the following format: 'I felt XX when you did YY. In future I would prefer it if you did ZZ'. Couching your response in terms of 'I' makes it harder for you to be passive, as you are owning your experience. It also makes it harder for you to be aggressive and blaming as you are not saying 'You did XX and it annoyed me because YY'.

Assertiveness is unlikely to be something you will be proficient at straight away. It usually improves with practice. You may have some setbacks as you acquire assertiveness skills but try not to dwell on them. The more you practice assertiveness the stronger your ability at it tends to get. It is usually the best way to get your needs met and you will be surprised at how effective it can be.

Question:

What does a good friendship look like and what does a toxic one look like?

Advice and Guidance:

Qualities of a good friendship include:

▸ Mutual respect, where each friend respects and adheres to the other friend's boundaries and limits

▸ If there is disagreement or conflict it is addressed constructively and respectfully

▸ You look forward to spending time with each other

▸ There is genuine reciprocity

▸ There is minimal or no gossiping and venting about each other outside of the friendship

▸ Neither friend is embarrassed or ashamed to be seen with their friend

▸ Each friend feels valued and respected by the other, so that no matter what their lives are like, they feel equal in the friendship

A toxic friend refers to somebody whose behaviour or their relationship with you is unhealthy or toxic. Toxic friends tend to create arguments and drama in the friendship. They can be very jealous and possessive. Signs you are in a toxic relationship or friendship include:

▸ You are afraid of them. For example, when you see a post or message from them on social media and you become highly anxious

▸ You feel very anxious and / or angry during or after interactions with them

- You feel they want you to 'fix' all their problems or rescue them

- You feel like you are being controlled by them or they are trying to control you

- You are afraid to upset them, like you are 'walking on eggshells'

Many toxic people have been through trauma themselves They may not be aware of how they are behaving or how their behaviour is impacting you or others.[5] Some behaviours which happen in friendships are not signs of toxicity, but they will require you to set some boundaries. These behaviours include things like:

- Controlling behaviour or asserting dominance over you. This is where your friend is often telling you what to do or criticizing you for doing things differently. Sometimes this is because the person assumes that they are acting in your best interests, in which case it is more paternalistic than toxic. However, once you are an adult, you can make your own choices and your own mistakes. In some instances, your friends really are looking out for you and not actually being controlling. For example, they take your car keys off you to prevent you from driving after you have been drinking alcohol or taking drugs. This is actually a demonstration of very good friend behaviour.

- Inappropriate teasing can become toxic, but it can be difficult to know what is friendly teasing and what is too much, as some people use teasing as a way to interact. Autistics can struggle to know when people are teasing in the first place, and many of my friends now know to tell me when they are teasing as soon as they have teased me. This is because I tend to take everything they say seriously and can become quite upset or confused by teasing of any sort.

[5] Source: psychcentral.com Accessed 7 January 2018

- Being critical of your way of doing things. Again, this can sometimes be because the way you are doing something is genuinely not sensible, for example if you are breaking a law that you didn't know about. In this sort of scenario, the friend is being a good friend. However, if the person does not respect any of your needs, such as telling you that you have to eat where they want, when you have a restricted diet, then this is not ok.

- Being overly demanding. Friends do ask for support from their friends, however, they should not be doing so all the time. A person that asks you to babysit their children regularly but does not do anything for you in return is being overly demanding and a toxic friend, so you are better off without them.

- Imbalanced power in the friendship. If you feel 'less than" the other person is the friendship, this demonstrates a power imbalance and signifies that the friendship is not genuine and healthy. It does not matter if one of you is rich and the other not, if one of you has high support needs and the other does not, fundamentally friends should feel as if they both contribute and are both valuable.

If you find yourself in a toxic friendship it is important to protect yourself. This will often involve severing ties with the toxic friend or setting and enforcing some very clear boundaries with them. Both autistic and non-autistic people can be toxic friends. Distancing yourself from the toxic friend can seem very difficult, and often results in some initial sadness, but the toxic friendship is something which is unhelpful for you and the toxic friend. There may be some 'fallout' from the friendship ending or from you setting boundaries. It is important to seek support if you are distressed by going through this process. As autistic people we often value friendship highly and losing a friend can seem a terrible loss but sometimes it needs to be done. Some toxic friendships can result in aggression, physical or emotional violence and / or re-criminations. Anyone who does those things to you is not a friend and you are better off without them in your life.

HOW TO LIVE WITH SOMEONE IN PEACE (MOSTLY)

This chapter includes tips to manage living with someone else successfully, including sharing space, money matters and navigating shared accommodation issues.

Question:

I want to leave home, but I can't afford to live by myself and I heard that autistic women are not able to live in private shared accommodation.

Advice and Guidance:

Many people move out of the family home and into shared accommodation, often with friends when they become adults. In many countries rentals are expensive and beyond the budget of students or young people who tend to work in lower-paid jobs or receive student payments. Shared accommodation can be a great step in independent living. However, a lot of difficulties and issues can arise in shared accommodation. These difficulties are not experienced just by autistics, all people can struggle to share living space with others at first.

Being prepared and understanding the sorts of things which can come up, especially interpersonal issues, and having some idea about the 'unwritten rules' of shared accommodation and how to avoid problems is really important.

This is a checklist of things to consider when looking for a shared property:

- Who you will be living with. You might have a friend or friends who want to live together with you or you may advertise for, or respond to an advert for a housemate. If you are sharing with friends you will probably have some idea of what they are like; their interests, whether and where they work or study, if they are a person who is careful with money or is more reckless and impulsive. When moving in together, these attributes can be very important, even if they weren't before you planned to share housing together.

- The location of the property; city or country, which suburb you might prefer, the proximity to your work or study and public transport, whether supports that you might need are available? These are all important considerations.

- The size of the property; taking note of the number of bedrooms and bathrooms and the cost and comparing that with your needs and available money is important.

- The amount of money you need to pay for rent. This is often the key factor in determining whether someone chooses to live somewhere, especially if they are in low-paid jobs or receiving benefits.

- How household bills and expenses will be split, this includes things like utility bills, water rates and landline phone and internet. Some accommodation provides these as part of the rent and others it is an additional expense. It is important to find out which BEFORE signing a lease.

▸ It is also important to decide who is going to put their name on the bills. This is important because the person with their name on the bill is responsible for paying it, even if they have moved out. It is important to know if your name is on the electricity, gas, water, phone or internet bill to ensure you change it over to one of the housemates who is staying on after you move out. Otherwise you may get landed with a big bill for services you didn't use, and have legal responsibility for paying it!

▸ Are you living with other autistic or neurodivergent people? This can be a lot easier as you can avoid the communication and cultural differences that exist between autistics and neurotypical people. However just because all your housemates are neurodivergent does not necessarily mean there will be fewer or no interpersonal issues in the share house.

▸ Whether there is a garden or not. Some tenants hate gardening and would prefer an apartment while some love gardens. In most rental agreements, the tenants need to look after the garden, so if you and your housemates are not able or willing to look after a garden it may be better to get an apartment with no garden to look after.

▸ Car parking spots. Many properties only have one carpark so if more than one housemate has a car this can be difficult. If this is the case, you will need to come to an arrangement of who gets to use the car park. It may be that the person who has the car park pays more rent than the rest of the people sharing the accommodation, which is reasonable.

▸ What time housemates get up in the morning and/ or go to bed at night. If you are a night owl and your housemates wake you up at 6 am this is likely to be an issue in the share house 'politics' and methods of ensuring people do not get woken up unnecessarily will need to be discussed before it creates animosity.

- ► Food preparation and payment. This may sound like a small consideration but in fact it is a very large one. How meal preparation is arranged; for example if each housemate takes it in turns to cook for the household, or whether all house-mates prepare their own meals or if there is some other arrangement. In addition, who is responsible for paying for food and what happens when a housemate takes something belonging to another person and eats it are the kinds of issues which can result in shared accommodation arrangements becoming very fraught and even ending. It is wise to discuss these issues either before or very soon after you move in together. Some people write their name on all their containers of food in the fridge and cupboards, whilst other people would find this quite offensive. Personally, I have lived in a variety of share arrangements, and when I was writing my name in whiteboard marker so that the 'thief' would have telltale blue hands, it was clearly time for me to move to somewhere I felt less of a victim!

- ► Cleaning the home is an important part of adult life, and some people hate/love cleaning. Many shared houses have a roster created by the house-mates listing all the chores which need doing to keep the house clean. This is generally a good idea although sometimes housemates may be lax in doing their allocated task. This situation requires the application of some assertiveness to ask the person to do their task. If a housemate knows that you will do their chores for them if they don't bother, they will probably stop doing them com-pletely. So, even if it is hard for you, don't do oth-er people's chores for them, unless they pay you to do so!

Sometimes you will have housemates leave and need to replace them. It can be hard to figure out whether or not someone will be suitable just by meeting them and having an interview/chat for half an hour or so. You can advertise for housemates in a variety of ways. There are real estate and renting sites online where you can advertise (or find) a vacancy. You will often need to pay a small fee to the website for this service. You can also tell your friends, family and any other networks you have that you have a vacancy. This can be a more effective way to source a suitable housemate as people you know can tell you more about the person than you are likely to glean from a website application. It is illegal in many parts of the world to specify that you want a specific type of flatmate.

Instead, you can specify the qualities that you would like in a future housemate and when you are interviewing new prospects assess them against this list. Each person will have a different list of desirable qualities. To help in developing your list consider what kinds of people you tend to get along with and what qualities they have, if you know.

You can look at the following sorts of attributes that you might like in a housemate:

▶ Neurodivergent / autistic, or non-autistics?

▶ Gender – male, female, trans man or trans woman, gender fluid or no preference?

▶ Introvert, extrovert, confident, shy?

▶ Creative?

▶ Student?

▶ Employed in a particular field?

▶ Preference for particular fandoms?

▶ Ordered and neat or chaotic?

▶ Particular faith?

- Particular ethnicity or cultural background (e.g. those who share your cultural background)?
- Vegan, vegetarian, gluten-free or not an issue
- And any other qualities.

The desirable qualities you choose do not need to be prescriptive, but they can help guide your decision. It is also a good idea to have another housemate involved in the interview or if you are the only housemate, a person's whose opinions and judgement you trust such as a friend or family member.

There are some warning signs that a person is likely to not be a good housemate for you. The main concerns include inability or unwillingness to pay rent or bills, bullying, exclusion or inappropriate and unwanted teasing, offensive or upsetting behaviour such as inappropriate sexual activity or harassment, theft from housemates or violence, or Illegal activity. Even things which are not illegal, but which are anxiety-provoking and unpleasant, such as housemates who do not work within how the household runs, can cause an unpleasant household. Things like playing loud music, particularly late at night, or getting up very early and making noise can be deal breakers for harmony in shared house situations. People who do not stop inappropriate behaviour even if you assertively ask them to do so can result in a lot of stress and misery. Either they or you need to move out. Sometimes, it is easier and more beneficial for you to move out, even though that can seem very stressful and a lot of hard work.

When you are looking for housemates there are some things which are a red flag for housemates who may make your life difficult:

- People who you dislike or feel uncomfortable around when you meet them

- People involved in criminal activity, drug use etc. There are different levels of this. Someone who illegally accesses overseas Netflix or has copied DVDs is probably not going to be a big issue, but those who are involved in more serious crime and drugs activity, such as dealing cocaine, can be very poor housemates. They are unlikely to disclose their criminal activities in the interview, although they might mention that they use 'recreational drugs'. If you are not good at spotting people who are a bit 'dodgy' then it can be helpful to have a friend or family member help interview prospective housemates as they may be better at picking people who may be involved in criminal activity.

- Couples; living with a couple can be very difficult, especially if their relationship is not going well. Couples can try to involve you in their arguments or dramas. If you aren't a fan of public displays of sexual affection, then living with a couple is likely to be something you would prefer not to do! However, it is important to note that people living in house shares can sometimes have sexual relationships with each other that can either work out or cause all kinds of drama.

- People who state strong views that are fundamentally opposed to your views. For example, opposing political beliefs, misunderstanding of disability and autism or inclusion generally, or those that have strong (anti)religious views. You don't want to spend your entire time at home avoiding topics or arguing!

- People who do not share your views in terms of the day to day running of the household, including frequency of cleaning the house, times they are active or noisy, preferences for TV shows or movies (especially if there is one TV in a shared area).

- People who are controlling or paternalistic. Once again having a friend or family member interviewing with you can help you see if there are issues in this regard.

Question:

What are some of the considerations you need to be aware of when moving into an established share house?

Advice and Guidance:

There are situations where you will need to move to another shared house. These include if the house you are living in is no longer available, such as if the property owner wishes to move into it or for someone in their family to move in or to sell the house. The property owner does need to give you and your housemates notice that this will occur, so you have time to find another house. Another reason you may need to move is if you do not get along with a housemate and it gets to a point where you feel you would be better off moving. Despite the most effective assertiveness and boundary-setting, sometimes you simply can't live with another person. You may also need to move to a different location to be closer to where you work or study.

It is worth making a list of attributes you are looking for in a shared house. Think about your concerns and preferences in a household. You can keep a checklist and when you have finished shared house interviews refer to it and tick off which positives and negatives each property has. Some things to be aware of when looking for another shared house include:

▶ Where are you planning to find your new home? Word of mouth from friends and family members can be a good approach, providing they know of suitable accommodation. Another way to find a shared house is through a real estate or share accommodation website. There may also be shared accommodation information available through your university or further education provider and if you work there might be shared accommodation information on your work intranet.

▸ When you go to shared house interviews to meet your prospective new housemates it can help to take a friend or family member along with you to notice anything you might not. For example, I once went to a share house where the bedroom on offer had a huge hole in the floor. This was so stunning to me that I didn't notice anything in the kitchen at all. I have also been interviewed for share houses where it became obvious that all the other people regularly took drugs. I may not have noticed that if I hadn't taken a friend with me.

▸ Pay attention to how tidy the house is. If you are very neat and it is messy, then that is an indication you might be unhappy, and end up spending a lot of your time cleaning! If the house is spotless and looks like a display home and you are a bit messy you may also have a hard time as your housemates might complain about your messiness.

▸ Financial imbalances are another potential issue. If you work full-time and your housemates are all students with no jobs or casual jobs, you may find yourself paying for more things than you want to and conversely if you do not have a large income and your housemates do, it can be difficult too. You can easily ascertain this in the interview by asking how the housemates spend their time, do they study or work?

▸ Remember that you are interviewing your new housemates as much as they are interviewing you. If you have questions or concerns about something, ask them.

▸ Ask how much the rent is and how it will be divided up between the tenants. In some cases, smaller rooms will have cheaper rent but in others rent will be equal for each room regardless of its size. However, it might be that some people share a room and this is ok, whereas in other share houses people who share a room need to make a bigger contribution to the bills.

- ▸ Ask about the household chores, how are they divided? Is it a roster arrangement where people take turns to do the same job, or is it an arrangement where individuals who have a preference for one or another job do that job all the time, or something else?

- ▸ Ask how costs for shared items are divided, for example cleaning products, laundry powder, toilet paper etc. It can become very annoying to find that you are the only person in the house replacing (and paying for) all these items.

- ▸ Ask what the arrangement for paying bills is, and how this works when flatmates move in and out regularly.

- ▸ Ask what sort of things the housemates do for enjoyment. This will help ascertain what life will be like in the house. If all the housemates are in a band and love playing music, it is likely that there will be late evenings filled with music. If the housemates are all members of the Young Labor Party, then you might expect that there will be a lot of political discussion and if the housemates are into craft then there will be a lot of knitting and sewing and so on.

Question:

What if there is conflict between my housemate and me?

Advice and Guidance:

A lot of autistic women struggle to deal with conflict and disagreements. It can result in us thinking the person will never speak to us again or that they will bully us or discriminate against us. Conflict can also be highly anxiety-provoking in and of itself. It can lead to meltdowns, shutdowns or self-criticism. Autistic women often actively avoid conflict. They can go to great lengths to avoid a conflict, such as learning all the likes and preferences of another person to avoid upsetting them, avoiding certain topics of conversation and pretending to think differently than they think. This is known as 'masking' in order to be accepted and it can come at the costs of autistic women's sense of identity and self.

Keeping up with avoiding conflict can also be exhausting and this emotional tiredness can impact on other areas of life. It can mean autistic women put up with a whole range of behaviours which need to in fact be called out and avoided; bigotry, dominance, bullying and even physical or sexual violence at the extreme end.

However, doing everything you can to avoid conflict is not a very useful long-term strategy. So, although it can be very challenging, it is better to learn some strategies to help manage your feelings in relation to conflict. Share house situations are a good place to do this, as conflict is very common in shared living.

Managing conflict and building assertiveness are related skills. Assertiveness is all about seeing yourself as worthy of getting your needs met and putting in place mechanisms to achieve that. Assertiveness is covered in detail in the previous chapter. Conflict resolution and managing conflict well are specific skills within the umbrella of assertiveness. Some useful strategies around managing conflict include:

▸ Telling yourself you are worthy of getting your reasonable needs met.

▸ Telling yourself that conflict is a natural part of human relationships. It does not need to escalate and having an argument is not necessarily a bad thing of itself.

▸ Being aware that conflict is sometimes a useful process to have with housemates, or indeed anyone. The value in conflict lies with the fact that after an argument both you and your housemate will have a better understanding of where each other is coming from. This can have the result of lessening conflict between you in the future.

▸ Be aware that every time you avoid a conflict you are essentially denying your housemate the ability to know your views. It can get quite out of hand if it goes on and they have no idea of your needs or wants because you have been pretending you don't have any needs or wants or that their needs and wants are more important than yours. This can result in meltdowns and outbursts as a release valve for all the angst the person has been holding onto.

▸ It is OK to tell your housemate if your needs differ from theirs. You are not being mean or rude. It is perfectly OK, and in fact it is a very good idea to set a boundary with others when you need to.

Question:

What do I need to know about money and shared living?

Advice and Guidance:

Living independently such as in share houses will mean you need to be responsible for managing your money; unless you parents or someone else is funding you but this is rare. The main expenses involved in shared accommodation include:

▸ **Rent.** This is likely to be a percentage of the rent

for the whole property you are living in. Often the rent is split equally between each housemate, but some share house arrangements have the person in the biggest room or who has access to some other perk paying more rent. The amount of rent you need to pay should be decided before you move in.

▸ **Food.** You are usually responsible for the food you eat. Each share house comes to its own arrangements around food but generally you can eat the food you paid for and not that of your housemates unless they give you express permission. It is not like being at home and taking something from the fridge.

▸ **Bills.** You will be responsible to pay for the utility bills, landline phone and internet, if you have them and they are shared at the property you live in. Usually there is a direct split between the utility bills and the number of housemates, so three of you sharing will pay 1/3 each of the electricity, gas and water bill. The Internet is generally split too, but if you have a landline phone and use it for calls, some shared households will add up any long distance or international calls and each housemate will pay their share of those. Once again, arrangements are different in different shared homes, but you need to ensure you pay for everything you are responsible for paying, and that you pay it on time.

Other things like sharing petrol and parking costs if you or one of your housemates has a car and shared usage of it with housemates will need you and your housemates to come to an agreement.

It is very important to ensure all these costs are paid on time and in full, or you can be breaking your lease agreement and be asked to move out.

Questions:

How do I know if I am being taken advantage of by my housemates?

Advice and Guidance:

Autistic women are frequently taken advantage of by unscrupulous people, including in shared accommodation. Signs that this is occurring include that your housemate/s are constantly asking you for money for things that aren't part of the expenses you all agreed on when you moved in, that you have a feeling that the expenses don't add up, or don't seem fair, and/or when you question your housemate/s on this they seem uncomfortable and they don't immediately have an answer.

Often people who are taking advantage of you will keep secrets about money. It can occur when you agree to move in. If you ask to see bills and your percentage is higher than it should be proportionate to the other housemates' or if the housemates flatly refuse to show you the bill, this is often a sign that you are being taken advantage of. Another sign you are being cheated is when you raise a concern and the housemates bamboozle you with confusing information. This is often used as a sort of smokescreen, to put the onus back on you to prove anything is wrong. Autistic women can be viewed as vulnerable or shy and unable to raise an issue. This can be the case even if you haven't told your housemates you are autistic.

It can be hard to raise this as an issue. You may feel it is likely that your housemate/s may become angry or accuse you of wrongdoing instead of them. In a shared house situation which is established, it can be very difficult to change the situation of being ripped off. Even though this is unfair, and it should not be you being punished, it can be easier and more cost effective to move out of the property rather than trying to get your money back and change the behaviour of the housemate/s. If you are just about to move in and these behaviours seem to be occurring, then it would be wise to decline the offer of moving in.

If you are in this situation you could try to assertively challenge the housemates, but one of the things that assertiveness does not work as well is knowing deliberate wrongdoing or criminal activity, so your assertiveness may backfire. One of the problems with this course of action is that you are still living in the property with the people you just challenged. If they have been intentionally taking advantage of you, they are not safe people. Life at home is likely to be very unpleasant in this situation and you may be anxious or afraid of recriminations and it is probably wisest to find another share house arrangement.

Some people feel guilty or foolish at being taken advantage of but there is no reason for this. The poor behaviour was by the people taking advantage of you. This is an experience which happens to a large number of people, and not only autistics. If you can, remind yourself the issue was with the people doing the wrong thing, not you.

In the end, if you are taken advantage of by housemates, it is awful but when it comes down to it, it means that you will most likely lose some money but the sooner you get out of the situation with the devious housemates the better. Chalk it up as a learning experience, say some choice swears at something inanimate (or whatever non-destructive thing you do to express anger) and find somewhere with people who respect and value you if you can.

Question:

I have lived in shared accommodation before but now I want to live with my sexual partner. Is it any different from living in shared accommodation?

Advice and Guidance:

Yes and no! It is similar to shared living in that you need to negotiate all the same things as have already been discussed in this chapter, such as who pays what, how the housework is divided up and who shops and cooks etc. It is different in that the dynamic between a couple is often more complex and difficult to navigate than house/flatmates. It is not a good idea to live with a sexual partner until you know each other quite well, as you do not want to ruin a good relationship just because you moved in together too soon. Some autistic women prefer to have a separate bedroom or even live completely separately from any sexual partners. For other autistic women, they can find it incredibly distressing if their sexual partner chooses to sleep separately. There is no right or wrong in general, so it is about working out what is right for you and your partner. If you cannot agree, then it is unlikely that your relationship will work out. See the chapter on healthy/toxic relationships to get an overview of the signs to look out for to avoid dangerous relationships.

TO DATE OR NOT TO DATE

HOW TO DECIDE IF YOU WANT RELATIONSHIPS OR NOT, PLUS PRACTICAL TIPS ON STAYING SAFE WHEN DATING.

Question:

I am interested in dating and hope to have a relationship, but my family tell me I shouldn't. Mostly I think this is because I am autistic, and they think autistics shouldn't date. What can I say to them?

Advice and Guidance:

As long as you are legally old enough, if you want to date and have relationships, you should have the opportunity to. Autistic people and people with disabilities generally should have the right to relationships and sexual expression if they want it. Your family may think they are protecting you from harm or being taken advantage of. While autistic women can be exploited by partners it is not reasonable to stop autistic women from dating. Teaching self-protection skills is far better than a blanket veto on relationships and dating!

In some societies there seems to be a taboo around dating and sex for people with disability. It may be that your family is caught up with that and are worried about the opinions and prejudice of others seeing you dating. The kinds of stigma around sex and dating for autistic people and people with disability more generally are very unhelpful. Whatever others say or think, you have the right to be in a relationship and to date if you want to. You might want to ask for dating and relationship tips from friends or supportive family members to help build your confidence.

Question:

My sister and my parents keep telling me I should start dating but I am very sure that I am asexual and a-romantic. I have no interest in sex, dating or relationships and I suspect I never will. But they keep dropping hints about 'settling down' and that 'there is a good man out there for you.' How should I respond?

Advice and Guidance:

While a great many autistics are interested relationships and sex, a great many others are asexual and have little to no interest in the kinds of 'conventional' sexual relationships. There is nothing at all wrong with this. It is natural. A great many neurotypical people are also asexual or choose celibacy. Many asexuals or celibate people can feel pressured by friends and family to start or stay in conventional relationships, so your experience is not uncommon.

Talking to family members about this can be difficult, especially if your parents are keen for grandchildren and you are an only child or one of a small number of siblings. You may need to explain your asexuality to them which can be difficult. It is best to be prepared for the conversation. Some topics to think about mentioning include:

- You are not waiting to meet the right person, you are happy without a partner

- You are not necessarily lonely or isolated

- Your asexuality is not necessarily a response to abuse or trauma

- Asexuality is a valid and common form of sexual expression   There are lots of asexual groups on-line, including asexual groups for autistics. (There is even an asexual flag.)

- Autistics are more likely than non-autistics to be asexual, and asexuality is common among the general population too, it is not a negative.

- Your asexuality has nothing to do with not wanting to give your parents grandchildren. It is part of who you are, not who anyone else is!

Question:

A number of people have asked me to date or have sex with them. I am not interested, but even when I say this, they still keep asking me. How do I manage this safely?

Advice and Guidance:

Generally, there are two types of people who are asking you, those who genuinely like you and are respectful of you and your wishes and then those who don't actually care what you think or feel. People who do not care what you think, or feel, are NEVER good to be in a relationship with and can often be quite abusive and dangerous if they don't get their own way. Because of this, it is advisable to handle the two types of people differently.

You can always try being polite but firm initially. For example; "No thank you. I don't want to come on a date/have sex with you." You do not have to justify your response, and if you try to explain why you don't want to go on a date or have sex, the other person may then try to talk you into it. If you are interested but not yet sure or ready, it is ok to say "Thanks for the offer, I am interested but can I take a rain check?" A rain check means that you want to do this later, just not yet.

However, if someone keeps asking you to the point it is annoying, they usually are not interested in what you actually think or feel. For these people, it is important that you keep yourself safe around them. For example, try not to be around them when there are no other people around, block them on your social media accounts. You may even need to block them on your phone and email.

Another way to stop unwanted advances (people trying to have sex or get into a relationship with you) is to say that you are already in a relationship with someone. If this is a lie, it is ok. If you do feel very threatened or vulnerable, you may want to take a self-defence class. Even though I am a pacifist, it is ok to hurt someone if it is to prevent them from sexually assaulting or physically hurting you. It is preferable to be able to just say no and walk away, but sometimes some people can become angry and even aggressive if they are rejected.

This is why it is really important to have a safety plan in place for when you do go out on a date and when you are starting a relationship. For example, when one of my friends meets someone from Tinder, they give me the person's name, phone number and place they are meeting (a public place) and a time by which they will be home or ring me to let me know they are ok. This means if they don't ring and don't get home I can give the police the relevant information.

Question:

I want to help my partner understand me as an autistic spectrum woman so that our relationship can be more successful. How can I do this?

Advice and Guidance:

All relationships take work and when everyone in the relationship understands their partner(s) that supports the relationship hugely. You may want to get your partner to read some general information about women on the spectrum, or if you are a transwoman, about trans issues. This can be a good starting point. If you have particular sensory sensitivities or communication differences, you may want to be very explicit about these.

Other really important information to share with your partner relates to time together and alone time. Many people on the autism spectrum need either more frequent or longer alone time after interacting and it is vital that no-one feels upset or hurt by this need. Communication is very important and it does not have to be verbal, you may choose to have conversations via email of whatsapp for example. Other people use music or art to share their emotional state. There is no right or wrong about how you interact as it is an individual choice, but it needs to work for BOTH/ALL of you.

Question:

What are some of the considerations around relationships for autistic women?

Advice and Guidance:

▸ There are a number of considerations for autistic women entering into and maintaining relationships. Many of these relate to difficulties understanding social expectations and the motivations of non-autistic partners. Some useful things to be aware of and which may help you to avoid some of the pitfalls which can occur include:

▸ Just because someone shows you affection does not mean you need to reciprocate it. Autistic women often enter a relationship because the choice of one is presented with little or no consideration of whether the relationship will be good or bad. You do not need to do this. Just because a relationship is offered does not mean you have to say yes.

▸ Some predatory people may try to enter into a relationship with you to take advantage of you - sexually or financially or for another reason. If your partner or prospective partner is frequently asking you for money or other favours without reciprocating or is acting in a controlling way towards you (such as managing all the finances in the relationship and giving you very little or no money and telling you what you can and can't purchase or do) this is somebody you should consider leaving as they are using you.

▸ If your partner discounts your experience or 'gaslights' you by making you doubt your own experience and thinking, this is somebody you are better off not being in a relationship with.

▸ As much as possible, don't use movies, TV and novels as your main source of information for dating and relationships. Autistic women can see something in popular culture and model their understanding of relationships and dating on this. Popular culture is not a good source of knowledge about dating and relationships regardless of whether it appears to be.

▸ Know that relationships involve give and take. If it is all one-sided then it is a relationship which is likely to fail or become very difficult – for example with one partner doing all the emotional support and when they have a crisis their partner is not available.

▸ Flirting is often a very confusing thing for autistics. We may miss it altogether or misinterpret it. Non-autistic people often expect everyone to understand their non-verbal cues so not picking up on these signals may send the signal you are disinterested – or interested even though you aren't.

▸ Dating another autistic or neurodivergent person is often a good idea given you are likely to have more things in common with them and share their approach to the world. However bad relationships can happen with neurodivergent or neurotypical partners alike. You may need to work on different sorts of issues than you would with a non-autistic partner to make the relationship work but there are likely to still be issues.

▸ It pretty much never ends 'happily ever after', despite what movies and TV shows say! Relationships usually take time and compromise, give and take and listening and arguments and selflessness and many other things in order to work. Fairytale endings belong in fairy tales!

Question:

Are relationships with another autistic or neurodivergent person easier than those with a non-autistic person?

Advice and Guidance:

Relationships are all different, even the way that you interact with a partner will be different depending on who the partner is. Other autistic people may find it easier to understand you and believe you when you are explaining your sensory sensitivities, but it might be that you need quiet to feel calm and your potential autistic partner needs noise to feel settled! A non-autistic partner may find it harder to understand you initially but may be just as capable of bringing you happiness and positivity.

Question:

Do you need to 'act' or hide your autistic self in order to be acceptable to prospective partners?

Advice and Guidance:

Most people, including neurotypical people 'act' to a certain degree when they start going out with someone. In the context of a traditional dating scenario, sharing details about your life, 'warts and all', tends to be seen as being a self-defeating way to begin a relationship because it can put people off you. The dating paradigm is almost like a job interview where you sell yourself to your prospective partner. While many people start their relationship by dating and gradually getting to know one another, this is not the only way to go about things. Some people know each other as friends first and then commence a relationship. Others meet in a particular setting and are drawn to one another and start a relationship. In these sorts of relationships acting is often not a good idea. Even if your relationships start through the traditional dating path there comes a time when acting is counterproductive. Your partner needs to know who you are, or the relationship is based in pretense.

Some autistic women are very accomplished social 'actors' and this is used to support their ability to manage in the mostly neurotypical world, like speaking a different language when you visit another country. This acting can become second nature, with women not noticing they are doing it, and it can carry across to relationships.

In any good relationship, honesty is a vital quality. Being able to express your likes and dislikes, things your partner does that bother you and even things like what music you enjoy can be hard for a autistic 'actor' to convey, We may be so self-conscious and insecure that we just go along with our partner's wishes and ideas even if we find them stressful, difficult of hurtful. This scenario helps nobody. If you are an 'actor' try to remember it is a coping strategy rather than who you are. You need to move beyond this in order to be honest and present with your partner.

It can be very difficult to be you if you are used to being a social chameleon. You may worry that your partner won't like you for who you are. You may even struggle to pinpoint what your likes are and what you want. Even if you explain this to your partner, it may be something they struggle to understand. Relationships with another autistic person can help you to avoid feeling the need to 'act.' While this is not always the case, an autistic partner may understand your experiences and approach to life better than a non-autistic partner and you may not feel the need to put on an act when around them. Conversely, when both partners are on the autism spectrum, this can create issues if anxiety, stress or distress in one person is felt and reacted to or then experienced by the other person, increasing the anxiety of the first person and so on!

Question:

How do you know if your partner is threatening or predatory or taking advantage of you?

Advice and Guidance:

Autistic women can be taken advantage of by a partner and not realise what is going on for some time. Predators and creeps seem to somehow have an ability to single out autistic women and take advantage of us in one way or another; sexual abuse and harassment, controlling behaviour, infidelity, bullying, gaslighting, theft are all things which happen to autistic women, often committed by those we love and trust. This is a terrible betrayal which results from the trusting and kind and helpful nature most autistic women possess. You might like to read Emma's book on relationships which looks at this in great depth (Goodall, E. (2016), *The Autism Spectrum Guide to Sexuality and Relationships*, London:JKP).

Some signs that a partner is predatory, disrespectful to you or controlling, include:

▸ They are controlling – telling you what to do, becoming angry if you do things differently to their wishes. This is an early warning sign and you should never stay with someone like this as it will never get better, and often gets far worse over time.

▸ They gaslight you. This is when somebody questions the way you experience things and often makes you doubt your sanity. Again, leave this kind of person before it gets worse.

▸ There is violence - physical, emotional or sexual. Even a violent act which seems 'small' is not acceptable. If there is violence in a relationship that indicates it is a toxic relationship and not one to save. Violence includes, but is not limited to:

▸ Sexual abuse - any unwanted sexual activity which you have not consented to or was forced on to you, this includes times when you were unable to give consent due to intoxication or being asleep or unconscious.

▸ Unwanted physical violence of any kind.

▸ Continual bullying and put downs; including being mean or rude about you in front of you to other people.

▸ Continual threats of violence or sexual abuse if you do not do what your partner wants.

▸ Unwanted restraint, physical or verbal, for example your partner forbids you from visiting friends or family. Again, this is a very big red flag for a very unhealthy relationship, which will usually progress to involve your partner being violent and aggressive to you. Another example is your partner preventing or trying to prevent you from accessing help for mental or physical health issues.

▸ Your partner controls all the money and/or takes all your money and does not give you any money for yourself.

   ▸ In all the above case - you should leave as things are highly likely to get worse, with most cases of domestic violence ending in murder having one of more of the above flags.

▸ Your partner becomes angry with you frequently and blames you for their emotional issues. This requires them to seek help from a counsellor, GP or psychologist. If they refuse to seek help then it is advisable to leave.

- Your partner is unfaithful, when you are in a monogamous relationship – this is a sign of disrespect and betrayal. Some couples resolve this issue, but it is a red flag for a number of other poor partner behaviours

- Your partner shares confidential information about you with others. They may not realize that this is not ok, so let them know you don't like this. If they still do not stop, look out for some of the other signs and if there are a number, you may want to end the relationship.

- Your partner is involved in crime or other unethical behaviour. If you know this under the law, in most parts of the world, you are also legally liable for their criminal activity. For example, if your partner steals things and they are in your home or car, even if only for a few minutes, you are harboring stolen goods, which is a crime.

- Your partner expresses that they don't want you to work or engage in social activities outside the home. If they forbid you from leaving the home, when they are out you need to phone a family member or friend or the police to help you leave.

- Your partner uses your autism diagnosis as an excuse to belittle and doubt you or your ability to work or parent or be a good partner. If they do not understand much about autism and they stop belittling and doubting you once they understand then that is ok, but if they do not stop then they are not valuing and appreciating you, so it would be advisable to leave them.

Question:

How do you end a relationship if it isn't going well or you feel uncomfortable or threatened?

Advice and Guidance:

If things are not going well anymore but you both still like and respect each other, you could seek counselling to try and make it work better. Counselling can help you both to clarify if you are better off together or apart. If your partner lies to the counsellor repeatedly, this is an indication that they do not value you. Bear in mind though, that two people interpret things quite differently, so they may think you are lying when you think they are lying. It is okay to break up with someone even if they like you, and some people remain friends with previous partners.

Breaking up is always more complicated if you have children and you need to think about where the children will live, whether custody will be shared or not etc. People can decide these things together, but it is always a good idea to have the details agreed legally, in case things get more fractious in the future.

However, if you have decided that the relationship is not healthy, and you need to end it, it is sadly important to have a plan as to how you end the relationship. This is because statistically speaking, leaving an unhealthy relationship can put you in physical danger. If you own property together and your partner is reasonable you may just be able to talk to them directly or through a lawyer about how to divide up your assets. If you are in social housing, you should talk to your housing officer or case manager. If you are experiencing domestic violence (being physically, verbally or sexually abused), seek help from a women's shelter or legal aid service. You can also apply to a protection order against your partner via the police and courts.

TOP TIPS TO UNDERSTAND AUTISTIC SPECTRUM WOMEN

AND HOW TO COMMUNICATE WITH THEM SUCCESSFULLY

Question:

My partner doesn't seem to understand me, how can I help them?

Advice and Guidance:

Whether or not your partner is also autistic or not, and no matter what their gender identity, most couples struggle to understand each other completely all of the time. Over time, with open and honest communication, understanding grows and develops. Even if your partner is also autistic, they will probably have a quite different presentation of autism to you and may well experience and respond to the world quite differently.

There are a number of factors that make up who we are, including our autism. Other factors include our gender identity, attitudes and values, religion or spirituality, age and health and auditory or expressive language difficulties. Our attitudes and values are the basis of how we judge the world and things within it, and this in turn can impact on what we communicate. How we communicate is impacted by our culture, our language skills as well as our sensory sensitivities and our emotional state. Your partner will also be impacted by all these factors and so you may both have similar or very different communication styles and content.

When we meet someone, we take time to get to know them and it can become apparent that difference, though not a barrier to a successful relationship can have an impact on understanding. If my spiritual beliefs have led me to follow a particular set of dietary rules for example, if my partner does not know about this, then it will be hard for them to understand.

Many autistics have a strong sense of social justice, which is not necessarily apparent to others immediately. This sense of social justice can drive our behaviour in ways that are bewildering to other people unless they understand our core values, for example; I believe that all living beings are equal in value, so I struggle to know what to do when people give conflicting instructions. Your partner may believe in a social hierarchy that helps them determine whose instructions are the ones to follow in the previous example. This can lead to conflict unless you both understand each other. Common misunderstandings arise due to differences in upbringing and different current attitudes and values. It can be useful to take time to explore together what each of your attitudes and values are in relation to the following:

▸ Society

▸ Children

- Relationships and friendships
- Politics
- Religion/Spirituality
- Animals
- Possessions/Money
- Housing
- Employment
- Autism/disability
- Sensory environment

When thinking about sensory environments it can help to be very clear about what types of sensory environment bring you the most joy, bring you the most calm and provoke the most distress in you. If you find loud music distresses you but your partner likes loud music and finds this relaxing, you will need to work out how to accommodate each other's preferences.

Sensory issues around food, clothing and smells can be very difficult for other people to understand if you do not explicitly communicate these. For example, if you find it horrendous to sleep in sheets that smell of a strong laundry detergent or softener, you may be grumpy if your partner has kindly done the laundry and put the clean sheets on the bed, but they have a very strong perfume, your partner will not understand why you are being grumpy and not appreciative unless you separate out the parts that you do and do not appreciate and help them to understand your sensory needs.

It is useful to develop your understanding of your own and each other's sensory preferences so that you can work out how to best interact with each other in supportive ways. This is particularly useful if you are going to, or do, live with each other. Even the colour of the walls can impact on some people's moods. If this is the case for you and your partner wants to paint walls a colour that will impact negatively on you, it is unlikely that they are doing this to upset or annoy you, and more likely that they are unaware of the impact on you.

Another area that can lead to misunderstanding is around the way each of you recognize and respond to your own emotions and those of others. If one of both of you has atypical interoception you may not recognize your own feelings and emotions unless they are really strong, or even have 'meltdowns' or 'shutdown' without really knowing that they were about to happen. This can make it harder to accurately recognize each other's emotions and so it is harder to respond in ways that you would each prefer. For example, if you are really sad, but your partner struggles to recognize their own sadness when things happen that could make them sad, it will be harder for them to see you are sad and respond supportively.

Difficulties with interoception are common in many people, not just autistics, and these difficulties impact on mood, behaviour and relationships. You can support each other by developing your interoception by actively noticing your internal body signals periodically throughout the day. Other ways to develop your understanding and responsiveness to each other are to use explicit signals or communicate about exactly what you want/need and why.

Be aware that not all people are nice and that if you have both tried all the strategies and tips above, and you still feel misunderstood all the time, you may need to evaluate the quality of your relationship. (See question on safe relationships).

Question:

Even though I have told my partner I need direct communication they still talk to me in ways that mean we have lots of misunderstandings. What should I do?

Advice and Guidance:

A key issue for autistics is that we interpret language literally, although even that is impacted by culture. So, if I hear someone say they need new thongs, my interpretation (literal) will depend on my culture; underwear (New Zealand), flip flops/rubber sandals (Australian) as well as whether or not I actually heard and processed the words. If I was emotionally overwhelmed or hearing a large number of other sounds at the same time, I may not even have actually processed those particular sounds, and so would have no interpretation to draw on. It can be very hard for non-literal language users to be literal, so it is important to use clarification as a communication aide. For example, if my partner said I need new thongs, I could ask them if they mean underwear or footwear. If I did not do this and I bought them footwear as a surprise, they may become frustrated with me if they actually wanted underwear!

A nice phase to help explain literal language is "say what you mean and mean what you say'. You can try asking your partner to do this and when they are unclear, ask them exactly what it is that they want. If you have additional auditory processing or expressive language difficulties, you may find texting or sms a more useful and direct way to communicate. If you use sign or AAC, you may need to teach your partner (or get them to learn from someone else) as a lack of fluency in these can lead to them miscommunicating by 'getting in wrong', in much the same way people make mistakes when learning a second spoken language.

Having an outsider support you both to communicate more clearly can also help. Apparently in the non-autistic world men are more direct than women and so some women may be communicating indirectly as they have been brought up that this is a polite way to communicate. For example, if a non-autistic woman says, 'it is hot in here', she may actually mean that she wants the air-conditioning on. If an autistic woman said the same thing, she is probably just describing her physical state. So, if you say that it is hot, and your non-autistic partner puts the air-conditioning on, even though you did not want it on, they are actually just anticipating your needs!

Question:

When I need alone time, my partner gets upset and says that I clearly don't love them. This is causing me a lot of distress; can we fix this or not?

Advice and Guidance:

This is quite difficult as both (or all) people in a relationship have needs, wants and desires. Where wants and desires conflict a solution that works for everyone is usually possible, but where needs conflict that can sometimes not be fixed. If you need a lot of alone time and your partner needs a lot of together time, that poses a difficult problem. Some people find a solution is to live separately or to live together but have separate living or sleeping spaces. What works for one relationship, may not work for another.

Many non-autistics find their emotional 'happy place' in socializing or being with the person they love. They can also be re-energized by interacting with other people. Many autistics on the other hand find quiet and/or solitude re-energizing. If you both (all) do not understand if these fundamental differences exist, you will have misunderstandings. However, if you are open and honest about why you both need/like/want alone time and together time, you should be able to work out if you are compatible or not. It may be that you can be friends but not in a relationship or you may find that actually you can find a perfect balance between together and alone time that suits you both perfectly.

It can help to both list:

▸ What I like about alone time:

▸ When I like to have alone time:

▸ What I like doing in alone time:

▸ What I like about together time:

▸ When I like to have together time:

▸ What I like doing during together time:

If, for example, you both like to clean the house together but one of you likes to grocery shop alone and whilst the other one has alone time, that can guide how you plan some of the practical aspects of being together.

Question:

My partner wants to have sex with me every day/night, but I am really not that interested, is it ok to refuse?

Advice and Guidance:

Your body belongs to you, not your partner. You always have the right to refuse sexual intimacy. In some cultures, it has traditionally been seen that a woman should submit to her husband but that is less accepted now and the law recognizes a woman's right to say no in most countries, whether or not you are married or in a long-term relationship.

People often have a differing level of sex drive (desire to have sex) and try to find a balance so that people both feel their needs and interests are being met. It may be that there are some sexual activities that you are more interested in than others. It may also be that your hormones are out of balance so that you are not interested in sex at all, or you may be asexual. Sometimes it is easier for asexuals to be in relationships with other asexuals, so that they avoid feeling pressured to have sex with someone.

Over time, people can find that their sex drive changes and they may lose or gain interest. It helps to talk to your partner about this and think of creative solutions to keep both of you content.

CHOOSING WHETHER OR NOT TO BECOME A PARENT

A DECISION MAKING SYSTEM FOR AUTISTICS

Question:

How can you decide if you want to be a parent?

Advice and Guidance:

The decision to bring a new person into the world should not be taken lightly. Your intentions and preferences around becoming a parent can change depending on time and circumstances. Sometimes people will be very against having children in their teens and twenties but when they get a bit older, they find they have a very different view about being a parent.

As we are mammals, we are subject to reproductive biological drives, like other mammals are. The will to reproduce is a primal, basic drive. However not everybody has a strong sense of this biological imperative, with some people feeling strongly that they do not want to reproduce. Deciding to have children or not can involve the basic drive to reproduce and some women instinctively feel that they need to be parents. Decisions around parenthood can also be based in a more considered method, such as assessing why or why not to have children. Even if you are someone who just 'knows' they need to be a mum, it is worth considering the reasons for and against having children.

Some factors to help make the decision around whether or not to have children include:

▸ Consider and quantify and write down (or audio record) the reasons why you want or do not want children.

▸ Are you single or in a relationship? There is nothing at all wrong with being a single parent but it can be more difficult, particularly around practical things like the household budget or managing with two or more children if one of them, or you, are unwell.

▸ Do you (and your partner) have support from friends of family should you need it – practical and emotional support?

▸ The nature of your relationship with your partner (if you have one). It is not necessary to have the stereotypical relationship in movies or novels but if you are in a relationship, a home of mutual respect and positivity tends to be a better environment to raise a child. Many people in non-traditional relationships raise children in all kinds of families.

▸ Consider the positives of having a child and then consider the negatives and how you might manage them.

There are some reasons that people bring a child into the world which tend to have negative consequences for the child and / or their parents. These include:

- To 'save' a failing relationship
- To 'trap' someone into marriage or staying in a relationship
- To access funding or benefits
- To avoid legal consequences (e.g. a criminal trial).

Red flags for a relationship which is not conducive to raising a child include:

- A relationship where there is physical, sexual or emotional violence
- A relationship where addictions are present – e.g. alcohol, illicit and / or prescription drugs, problem gambling etc.
- A relationship where criminal behaviour is going on
- A relationship where there is no love or connection (although noting that autistic people often experience and demonstrate love differently to the 'norm')

The pessimistic view of parenting is that a child is a lifelong commitment. A child of any type can have a wonderful journey through life, or they can really struggle. Children can sap energy and when young require huge amounts of attention and time as well as a lot of money to raise. Even your level of freedom will be impacted by having children with not just your needs to think about but theirs too. Even when you are having a horrible day, your child may need your love and support to help them through their own horrible day. Your child will look up to you as their main influence and role model, often for many years, or even forever, so if you fail at something it can make them anxious and disillusioned. They get sick and then you get sick and have to look after them while feeling unwell yourself. Children, especially those on the autism spectrum, expect you to always be 'fair' and make no mistakes or say or do anything inconsistent.

Over a number of years, your child will probably be watching movies and TV programs and listening to music that you really don't like, which for some autistic people can actually be highly distressing. Your child's emotions, meltdowns and setbacks will have an impact on you (and/or your partner). You will probably be highly anxious about their difficulties, illnesses, failed friendships and disappointments. When your child becomes a teenager, another stressful stage for parents, it is reasonably likely your teenager will at some stage be rebellious and difficult. Although this is an important stage in the development of identity and self, for parents it tends to be quite unpleasant,

The optimistic view of having children is that you are bringing a person into the world and you get to shape their future in a positive way. There is nothing that compares with the love of a child for their parent/s and vice versa. You may be able to see the world through their viewpoint of innocence, which can be an amazing experience. Your child is likely to always have a strong emotional bond with you and may call you mum/mother/mummy, which may be a powerful emotional grounding for you. Even for people who don't connect much with their emotions, love for your child can be an immensely powerful and moving state.

Some parents find is highly rewarding to use their experience of life and understanding to support a child and guide them onto a positive path. If your child is autistic, or even if they aren't; you can use your own experience of the world to support their journey. You can be their strong defender, role model and as they grow to adulthood, be their friend. Many parents find that children give them a huge sense of purpose and a meaning in life.

Biologically and evolutionarily speaking, raising a child actually is our prime purpose as humans. We came down from the trees a fair while ago but those homo sapiens' survival instincts still persist, which is why despite all those challenges and difficulties, most people still want and have children. It is testament to the value of parenting that very, very few parents will ever make the choice to give their children up, even if life is really difficult. However, for parents that do choose to place their child(ren) up for adoption, this is usually done out of a strong desire to give the child(ren) the best life possible.

Deciding whether or not to have a child is a decision which may take a lot of consideration, not just writing a pros and cons list, looking at it and saying 'I pick this option!' It is a decision to discuss with your partner if you have one and maybe with friends who are parents themselves, preferably autistic friends as their experience is likely to be closer to yours than the experiences of neurotypical parents.

Question:

Do you have to be in a relationship to be a parent?

Advice and Guidance:

It is not essential to be in a relationship in order to be a parent. Often women become single parents due to a relationship breakup or not being in contact with their child's father. While there is a stigma about being a single mother in some countries or cultures, it is the most typical form of parenting in others. Being a single parent is not something to feel shame about and there is no excuse for others to judge single parents. However, in many countries the logistics of being a single parent can be quite daunting. If a mum works, her child will need to be in commercial childcare or looked after by an extended family member. Some childcare is subsidized by some Governments or provided by some employers, but this is not the case for everyone. Childcare can be very expensive and if children do not cope well with being in childcare, then a single mum is left with the difficult choice of whether to go to work and have an unhappy child, or to not work and struggle more financially. Child care provided by extended family members or friends can be a great solution. However, these arrangements can change and fall through for a variety of reasons.

For autistic women, the anxiety around working and finding suitable childcare can be significant. Having a partner around can also take away some of the stress from parenting. You can leave your child with your partner and leave the house if you need space or solitary time. Being a single parent means you are likely to be with your child or children all or most of the time. Even if you work you will spend your non-work time with your child. For some parents this is fine but for others it can be very stressful and they can crave time alone and/or adult company and activities.

Some of the positives around being a single parent include that you may forge a very strong bond with your child and if the reason you are single was to escape a violent or abusive partner then you did a great and necessary thing to protect yourself and your child from that person. Many autistic women struggle to be in a relationship due to a rage of factors and this can mean that with all the logistical challenges and potential stigma, that they are much happier raising their child or children without a partner. Some autistic women may have a more informal and non-traditional relationship, for example one where they live in different locations to their partner and only see each other infrequently. This can result in child care arrangements which may be effective but look a bit different to the expected. It is important to know that as long as they are raised in love and care - whatever that means for them, in an environment free of violence of any kind, that their health care and material needs are met, and have the opportunity to engage in education, then anything else related to how many parents there are or what the parenting relationship is completely irrelevant.

Some countries provide IVF treatment to single and/or lesbian women to help them conceive a child of their own, whilst others do not. Where this is provided, it can be extremely expensive, and where it is not women can struggle to find a person willing to donate their sperm. Gay men (single or partnered) have formed non-traditional families with lesbian women and couples to raise children in a way that ensures a number of adults are able to share parenting duties. Non-binary, gender questioning and trans people can all make wonderful parents and may or may not be able to access medical support to do so.

Question:

What are some of the challenges that autistic mums face?

Advice and Guidance:

While parenting can be an amazing experience and raising children to live the best lives they can is a wonderful thing to do, there are some challenges which autistic women can face as mums. These include:

▸ Autistic women often have sensory processing issues which can be triggered by their child's actions. Autistic women may be highly anxious parents, worried and catastrophizing over things which others may barely notice.

- ▸ Setting and maintaining boundaries with their partner and children may be challenging for autistic mothers.

- ▸ Autistic mothers may be dismissed, ignored or discriminated against in childcare, school and other domains.

- ▸ Some autistic women may come to the attention of child protective services - not for actual abusive behaviour against their children but because something seems 'odd' to neighbours or medical/education staff. Difference in parenting styles from the dominant cultural norm is often not respected or even acknowledged.

- ▸ Autistic mums of autistic kids are often a great mix but in a household full of autistics, meltdowns, low mood or stress can spread like contagion due to the hyper empathy often experienced by many autistic people.

Question:

Someone whose opinions you value tells you autistic women shouldn't have kids because they can't look after them. Is this true?

Advice and Guidance:

Put simply no, this is not right and nor is it true. Autistic women can look after children just as well as neurotypical women can. There are exceptions to this amongst both autistic and neurotypical mothers. Some autistic mums are managing well as parents as are some neurotypical ones and some are not capable of taking care of kids, whether their own or other people's; either in the short or longer term. This is the case for both autistic and neurotypical parents. In fact, most parents regardless of their neurology are neither exemplary nor awful, they are doing the best they can. They care for their kids and want the best for them and they will do everything they can to ensure their child grows up happy and healthy and free from trauma and danger.

Autistic women have as much right and capacity to be mums as their neurotypical peers. The issues that autistic women can experience are often a bit different from the kinds of issues non-autistic women experience. Autistic mothers often bring a range of positive aspects to their parenting. For autistic children having an autistic parent is often a wonderful thing, enabling them to be accepted at home and learn their skills at life from someone who shares their understanding of the world.

The concept of autistic women all being negligent parents is rooted in a long-standing area of ableism and discrimination focused on the idea that Disabled people don't need and are not capable of relationships and so can't parent. Sadly, there are too many true stories like the ones about women with intellectual disability sitting in a doctor's waiting room to get their dose of contraception so they wouldn't have children they apparently couldn't care for, forced sterilization of women with all manner of disabilities to 'spare' the world from the disabled offspring they might have, and accounts of young women with disabilities having puberty halted so they never reach physical maturity are sadly widespread. These types of practice continue to this day, though will less regularity and less widespread acceptance. Forced sterilization is recognized across the world as a human rights abuse.

Negative attitudes around sexuality, parenting, gender and disability are so pervasive in some cultures/countries, that when autistic women talk about wanting to be parents, many people, even apparently educated and respectful people, often question the capacity of autistic women to parent. In this situation, being an autistic parent may have become a political statement, simply through the natural and common practice of having a child.

However, for some autistics, just as for some non-autistics, parenting is not something that they want to engage in due to a variety of reasons, such as an aversion to the sound of babies/children crying or a need for large amounts of quiet time/solitude. Whatever your decision, it is your decision, which though it may or may not change over time, should be respected by others.

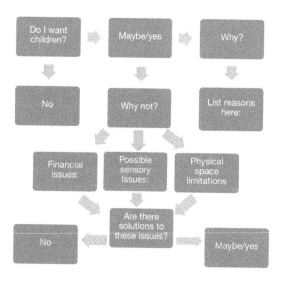

BEING AN AUTISTIC PARENT

Becoming a parent is one of the most profoundly life-changing events a person can have. Children bring great joy, immense love and often a range of practical and emotional challenges. For autistic women, having a child can bring with it not just the anticipation of a lot of joy but also a lot of anxiety about what baby might change about day to day life. Autistic women can face some additional challenges around parenting, many of which are related to perceptions of them and their parenting style from other people, rather than inherent difficulties.

It is important to note that more pregnancies end in miscarriage than are carried to term. Only about 15% of all pregnancies result in a live birth. Many women do not know that they have miscarried as it may seem to be a very heavy period in the early weeks of a pregnancy. After twelve weeks of pregnancy the likelihood of a miscarriage significantly decreases. This is why many people do not tell anyone about a pregnancy until after the twelfth week. Sadly, there are still pregnancies that do not result in a live birth and this can be very distressing for the mother and their family.

Question:

How can I have children?

Advice and Guidance:

When you decide to have children, you will need to work out how you are going to do this. For some women, becoming pregnant is very easy. Unprotected (no form of contraceptive being used) sex (penis ejaculating into vagina) is required to conceive a child 'naturally'. However, some women use a sperm donor who ejaculates into a container, the sperm is then inserted into the woman's vagina using a syringe or 'turkey baster'.

Other women seek IVF or other assisted conception from medical services. These are free in some countries and cost a significant amount of money in others. If you are a transwoman it is likely to be impossible for you to carry a child (be pregnant) but if you have some of your sperm frozen earlier in life, a child could be genetically yours if you chose to use the sperm with your partner's egg or another woman's egg.

Pregnancy is only likely to occur for a short period of time in a woman's monthly cycle, but it is quite hard to predict with 100% accuracy. Some women who have been told that they or their partner are infertile (unable to become pregnant) do actually become pregnant. It is useful to talk with your GP if you have been trying for over a year without success to become pregnant.

It is also important to note that you can become a parent without giving birth. You can parent a partner's child(ren) or adopt or foster children. All of these are equally valid. It is not true that you love 'your own more', if a child comes into your life and you are happy about this, then love is love.

Question:

How and when should I prepare for a new baby

Advice and Guidance:

There are two main areas of preparation; emotional and practical/logistical. It is a good idea to start preparing for the arrival of your baby once your pregnancy has been confirmed at or after 12 weeks. You may still want to discuss your pregnancy with your partner or close friends/family prior to that but be prepared that the pregnancy may not continue to full term (live birth).

Logistical requirements for having a new baby include:

▸ Getting all the things you will need when the baby is born; somewhere for baby to sleep, for example a cot or a bassinet, as well as clothes and nappies for baby – be sure to look at the costs involved in both cloth and disposable versions. You do not need things like a change table, rather you can have a change mat that you can use wherever you are.

▸ Babies need stimulation to grow and develop, so they should have some toys and books. However, babies do not need lots and lots of expensive toys and are often happy exploring inside and outside with you and playing with household items like pots, boxes and wooden spoons.

▸ Find a room or space in your house for the baby to sleep. Babies need their own bed/cot/place to sleep as it is very dangerous for them to sleep in bed with you. Damp, smoky or overly hot spaces are not good for babies to sleep. Some families have a baby sleeping in a cot or bassinet next to mum's bed and others have a baby in their own room.

▸ Learn how to take care of your baby - this could involve going to prenatal or antenatal classes, reading pregnancy and baby books and / or talking to close friends or family members who are also mums.

More intangible considerations for new parents include:

▸ Talk to friends or family members about parenting, what it involves, what the issues can be, what you need to know etc.

▸ Be aware that you will almost certainly be more anxious when the baby comes along and put in place some strategies to manage your anxiety. When one of the authors first worked with babies, she was so worried that one of them would stop breathing during nap time that she was checking their breathing constantly.

▸ If you are having a second child (or third, etc.), prepare your older child for what to expect. Be aware that they may be upset or jealous at the arrival of a new sibling, or they might be delighted. Make sure to let them know that the baby will require a lot of your time and energy but that you will still have love and time for them.

▸ Be aware that sleep will almost certainly be impacted by the arrival of a baby. This can continue for many years so working out some strategies to address this issue can be very helpful, particularly given autistic people often struggle with sleep anyway. If there are two or more adults in the family, it can help to plan who will get up to feed or calm the baby in the night when the baby wakes up distressed.

- A range of factors around birth and parenthood can impact on mental health. Postnatal depression and less frequently postnatal psychosis can happen to any mother and can make life very hard, especially for single mothers and / or those who have children already. If you struggle with alexithymia (emotion blindness) it can be difficult to notice if things start to get difficult. It is worth asking someone close to you to tell you if they notice any changes in your outlook and approach following the birth of your child. This could be your partner, a close friend or a family member. Regular contact with your GP is a good starting point to keep a caring check on you and baby.

Question:

What kinds of practical issues are there around having children (e.g. costs, impact on lifestyle of parent/s, space and safety requirements)?

Advice and Guidance:

The costs of having a child are significant and include ongoing everyday costs like diapers / nappies, clothes, shoes, formula / baby food etc and then one-off costs like a car seat, cot, bassinet, bed for when they get older and furniture for their bedroom. There are also education costs: school fees/contributions, child-care, cost of school trips and excursions, school uniforms, transport, books, stationery. Medical costs will vary from country to country but include; doctor visits, specialist appointments, medication, vaccinations, dentist visits. Finally, there are additional costs for extras such as music lessons, sport, hobbies and interests.

This is not to say you will need to come up with a

huge sum of money as soon as you bring your baby home but there are many ongoing costs which will occur over the length of your child's childhood and adolescence. In addition, if your child is born with or develops a significant disability some of these costs can become much higher. Other costs are emotional and energy. For example, if your baby doesn't sleep through the night for 18 months, that is 18 months of disrupted sleep patterns which can take a lot of energy and an emotional toll.

Children's impact on their parent/s' lifestyle can be significant. Raising a child takes a lot of time and attention. You can't really say 'I just parented for three hours. Now I'm having a break!'. Children vary hugely in terms of their temperament, emotional and psychological make-up, ability to entertain themselves and many other factors. This can make a big difference in terms of the experience of their parent/s. Autistic parents can really struggle with personal space and energy levels and feel they need a lot more physical or emotional space than they actually have. A child who wants to tell you EVERYTHING they are doing all day, who is very extroverted can be a real challenge for an introverted, quiet autistic mum. Just as challenging can be a child who shares none of your interests and passions! Children do not come with an off switch, although they do sleep it is not always for more than a few hours at a time, so developing some strategies which work for you to have some 'me time' can be helpful.

For many parents of young children, the only time they get to themselves, except for sleep, is when they go to the toilet. It is ok to close the bathroom door and take an extra five minutes for yourself, just to breathe and be in stillness before rejoining your family.

Sometimes the issues parents face might seem trivial but are in fact very difficult to manage. Children and their parents tend to enjoy different TV, movies and music. For a parent who is highly musical and has perfect pitch and for whom listening to a particular type of music is one of their favourite things, having to endure children's music day in, day out, can be overwhelming. The trick with lifestyle issues is often to acknowledge they exist and try and work out ways to approach the situation which support both you and your child, such as you or your child listening to their music on headphones or designating quiet time when needed for both you and your child.

If you like to eat particular foods and your child does not, this can also create difficulties. Friends who do not have children may not want to spend much time with you once your child is born or may just talk about your child rather than you. Some mothers feel that a part of their identity is lost once they become 'a mother', and that people see this before they see them. Once your child starts preschool or school, you will be spending a lot of time taking your child to and from places where there are lots of other parents and children and this focus can be difficult for some people, whilst other mums really enjoy this lifestyle.

The cost of children also impacts on lifestyle as it means that you have less disposable income to spend on other things in life, like going out for new clothes or spending money on your passions and interests. This cost is ongoing as food costs increase as a child grows, however clothing costs can decrease over time particularly if you recycle or upcycle or make your own clothes for them/the family.

Question:

My parents said I had no sense of danger as a child, how will this impact my parenting?

Advice and Guidance:

Children, and especially small children, usually have a different understanding of risk and safety to their parent/s. Children are less likely to know the consequence of running into the road or swimming by themselves. It is up to parents to manage risk on behalf of their kids and explain consequences of risky behaviour at least until the children are old enough to regulate their own safety. This is particularly true for autistic children who may be keen to do something and not be aware of the potential danger. In addition, because autistics have atypical interoception they are not always able to read and respond to body cues, putting them at further danger.

For example, if your child does not read their body cues for air hunger when their head is underwater, this places them at greater risk of drowning. In this case, not only do you need to teach them to raise their head above the water whenever they are in the bath or any water, but until they do so automatically, you should never leave them in water alone. Other body cues that may not be read and responded to are temperature, so you child may go blue but not want more clothes on, in which case you need to tell them that it is cold and that they need more clothes on to keep their body warm and working well. They may need to be told to drink as they may not have a sense of thirst. Mindfulbodyawareness.com has some resources to provide you with more information about how to help children (and yourself) develop your interoception to help you and them to develop the skills to self-manage and self-regulate.

It is not only your responsibility as a parent to physically protect your child but also to teach them to be able to recognize danger and consequences as they grow. Some autistic parents can become, often quite understandably, highly anxious and not want their child to be exposed to any danger. The problem with this is that a child shielded from every possible risk or disappointment can become an adult that is terrified to do anything and lacks independence or resilience, which is obviously not a good outcome. The key is to be aware of potential danger and shield your child from that but also to have some realistic perspective about potential consequences. This means a parent can know what to protect their child from and what to support them to have a go at and hopefully build their knowledge of danger and consequences and the ability to make informed choices about what risks are OK to take and those to avoid at all costs. Age and maturity level are important factors in children understanding safety and risk.

Although stranger danger is a well-known phrase, most danger is from people who are known. It is better to teach your child about safety and trust and to allow them to say no to physical touch from a young age. They should also be taught how to let you know if someone tried to/did touch them without their consent. This is particularly important if your child does not (yet) speak.

Question:

I shared a room when I grew up but my partner says babies have to have their own room? Are they right?

Advice and Guidance:

You may well need peace and alone time and your child's needs may be similar to yours or very different, with them having a strong preference for being able to see or touch you at all times. Maintaining appropriate space for yourself and the other members of your family can be quite a challenge, especially when each person's needs are at odds.

Some children are happy to share a room with their sibling(s) and others are not. Some children will be happier alone in their bedroom while others will stay in communal areas in the house and talk to everyone who is there! If you are a quieter and more solitary type person this can be quite challenging if your child(ren) are louder and more social. However, for more social parents, it can be disconcerting to have a child who prefers alone time and spends most of their time in their bedroom reading, drawing or playing.

Some children, especially autistic children, like to have a safe space that they can retreat to, such as inside their wardrobe or under/in their bed. Parents may not have the money to provide a totally private quiet space for their child so may need to think creatively about how to find a space where their children can have some quiet time to themselves and feel safe and protected. One child's needs for space may encroach on the needs of another person in the household. This is an area for flexibility and lateral thinking where possible.

For most people it is simply not an option to live in a bigger place or to make renovations to their home to accommodate everyone. However, for autistic people, adults and children, space considerations can be incredibly important and help them to manage other things which may not seem related, but which are impacted by needs for space and alone time. It is a good idea to discuss space requirements with your family, and your partner if you have one. Try to identify your own needs for space. This may be difficult, particularly if you struggle to identify or articulate your own emotions or needs. Perhaps each door can have a 'do not disturb/its ok to knock' sign which occupants can hang up to let other people know if they are having quiet time or are ok to interact. The bathroom should also have one of these!

It is always important for parents to remember that

they cannot assist their children if they are struggling with life themselves. It can help to remember the safety demonstration on airplanes where the flight attendant advises that if there is a loss of cabin pressure passengers should fit their own oxygen mask before attending to their children. Parents usually struggle with this issue and are often willing to ignore their own needs for the sake of their children. If this pattern continues then the consequence is likely to in fact be worse in the long term for children than the short-term loss of attention from parents looking out for themselves too. This is true when thinking about your own needs for space and quiet time.

One strategy involves you thinking about your reaction to being in different spaces in your home when you are with yourself, and then when the other members of your household are around. Try to notice if you feel uncomfortable, peaceful, angry, physically 'tight' or stressed and make a list of situations and places where you feel comfortable and calm as well as those where you are unhappy and struggling. This can help inform the discussion with your household about managing space. Depending on your children' age, cognitive ability and maturity you can ask everyone in the household to do the same exercise and then together come up with a plan to help ensure people can have alone time or tie out when they need to.

School age children are often overwhelmed when they arrive home and need time to 'recharge'. For some children this recharge requires peace and quiet, others a particular noise and/or activity and for others social interaction with a particular person or people or a specific animal. There is no way to know what will work for a child in advance as each child is different.

Question:

What do autistic parents tend to do really well?...
and not so well?

Advice and Guidance:

It is important to note that as with all people, autistic
parents are often vastly different from one another.
There is no definitive autistic parenting style. However, there are some general strengths and challenges which autistic parents tend to experience. Autistic
parents tend to have great skills in some areas of parenting, including:

▸ Being a strong ally and confidante for their children

▸ Bonding very closely with their children, especially their autistic children   Being innovative and
creative parents

▸ Having a more logical, rational approach to life.
This has many potential benefits in parenting

▸ Less likely to be judgmental.   Accepting their
children for who they are regardless of sexuality,
gender identity, ideas, mental illness, or any other attributes which non-autistic parents can find
disconcerting

▸ Autistic parents are often very thoughtful and try
to see things from their child's experience

▸ Autistic parents often view their children as small
human beings with their own rights, beliefs,
character and approach to the world. An autistic
parent is probably less likely to infantilize or con-
descend to children

▸ Having a strong sense of their responsibility as
parents   Being genuine, honest and trustworthy

▸ Not 'sugar coating' life lessons or hiding things

from their children

Autistic parents tend to find some elements of parenting difficult. This does not mean that all autistic parents will struggle with the things as, like all parents, autistic parents are individuals. Some of the difficulty autistic parents may experience include:

▸ Their own difficulties, for example sensory issues or overload, can make it more difficult for them to 'be there' for their kids at times

▸ They can struggle with setting and maintaining boundaries and limits with their kids

▸ If children are having a meltdown, shutdown or experience something which their parent finds triggering, it can be hard to manage and may set off traumatic memories or triggers for the parent

▸ Arguments and fighting between siblings can be triggering. Parents can find it hard to address the sibling behaviour but can also find it triggers their own anxieties around conflict

▸ High anxiety is a common experience for most autistic people. Having a child, on one level, essentially involves a lifetime of worrying about their safety. This can make life very challenging for autistic parents and impact on their ability to support their kids to take controlled risks or take on new things.

▸ Autistic parents can experience a lot of self-doubt and self-criticism. This is often in response to external criticism.

▸ If their children are non-autistic there can be a disconnect between parent and child.

▸ Their honesty can be difficult outside of the family. For example, if an autistic parent tells their young child there is no Easter bunny and Santa Claus isn't real and the child tells it to everyone at school and other parents are upset by this.

▸ Autistic parents can sometimes be inflexible to their child's needs and wishes if they themselves don't share them (however, this is a fairly universal difficulty encapsulated in the saying that children should be seen and not heard).

Question:

What are the benefits for autistic children of having an autistic parent?

Advice and Guidance:

Autistic children can benefit greatly from having an autistic parent for a variety of reasons. An autistic parent can have a shared understanding of the world with their autistic child. Autistic parents tend to have life experience of many things which their autistic children will also experience, so they can provide helpful and relevant advice and support to their child. Autistic parents can be incredibly close to their autistic children. An autistic parent can be their autistic child's strongest supporter and advocate as they grow, and they can act as a communicator or interpreter for their child around interactions with non-autistic adults, for example a classroom teacher the child may be having difficulties with.

Question:

I have had a lot of criticism and unhelpful 'advice' from some non-autistic parents telling me I am doing it 'wrong' but my child trusts me, and we have a great relationship. It's just that we do things a bit differently. What should I do about this?

Advice and Guidance:

Sadly, the experience behind this question is quite common for autistic parents, who can feel judged by other people. We live in a world where autistic experience is in a minority and is either not acknowledged or understood or it can even be criticized as 'weird' or wrong. We also live in a world where there are a wide variety of opinions around effective parenting.

Some people dismiss or disrespect the experience of autistic parents. Combine that with your autistic child experiencing difficulties, or just acting in a different way to their peers, and you have the recipe for some significant judgement levelled at autistic parents. This is not actually a reflection on your capability as a parent at all and more a reflection that people can be narrow minded and judgmental and that often people can jump to conclusions based on a very small amount of evidence rather than gathering all the facts. In this situation it can be the case that knowledge is powerful, and the person might change their views with a bit more understanding about autism, in general or specifically in relation to you or your family, but that is not always the case.

It is best to remind yourself that you are doing the best thing for your child and if you want advice seek it out from a friend or family member who you trust and who respects you and try to ignore the people who criticize. If you are confident enough, let the critics know that you don't really want or need their input! It is important to bear in mind that parenting styles are often based in socio-cultural norms, so your style will just be one of many amongst local parents.

Question:

What are the differences between autistic and non-autistic parenting styles?

Advice and Guidance:

There is no accurate answer to this question, as all parents are different and parenting styles are influenced by socio-cultural norms of what it means to be a parent or child and the roles and values that each 'should' have. For example, there are helicopter parents and tiger parents, to name just two common parenting styles.

Children require love and opportunities to explore their environment and that of the wider world and to develop communication skills (of whatever kind suit them). With these, all other variables are just that, variables.

Question:

I have been told I will never be able to bond with my child because I am autistic. Is that correct?

Advice and Guidance:

If you give birth to a child, you may or may not automatically bond with them. For some parents (biological or not) the first time that they hold their baby/child is magical, for others it is not. It does not mean that you will never bond with your child if you do not have that magical moment.

In addition, when mothers experience postnatal depression, this can seriously impact on their ability to bond with their baby until the depression is managed. For other mothers, the birthing experience is so traumatic or overwhelming that they require some down time before being able to feel a bond with the baby.

Having regular check-ups for mum and baby are important to ensure that no physical or mental health issues are preventing growth and development for baby and well being for mum.

PLANNING FOR OLD-AGE AND/OR ILL-HEALTH

Autistic women need to plan for their old age and/or ill-health so that it is as easy as possible when the time comes. Considering that we are all going to die, and most likely either become old and/or suffer from ill-health at some stage in life, many of us have not planned for these stages in our life. For example, planning for old-age is not just about planning for the end of our lives, such as organising our funeral or writing our will. Indeed, planning for old-age involves working out and writing down or otherwise recording your plans and wishes for how you want to live as you get older.

For example, some people may wish to live in supported accommodation or retirement villages, whilst others may wish to stay in their own homes as long as possible. Even if you wish to stay in your own home as long as possible, you may need to make plans for if you become unable to manage in your own home. If you have children, you may assume that day will be able to take care of you, or that they will not take care of you. You should avoid making assumptions and should instead utilize the logical detailed planning skills that so often go with being on the spectrum to create a comprehensive document detailing your wishes.

Depending on where you live, different laws govern different legal aspects of ageing or becoming unable to manage your own financial, physical, mental and/or emotional well-being. Part of your planning should relate to legal aspects such as: guardianship, power of attorney, living wills, whilst the rest of your planning will cover things not governed by legal paperwork.

In general, you will need to be thinking about yourself and any other dependent family members. These dependent family members could be older than you, of a similar age, or younger. They may be parents, spouses or partners, children or other extended family members. If you have pets, you should also record who you wish to take care of your pets if you are unable to do so.

For many autistics, the idea of living in residential accommodation and leaving their own home is incredibly frightening. However, unless you can afford 24/7 care in your own home, there is a possibility that you may require supported residential accommodation prior to dying. Planning for this eventuality, is as much about giving service providers the information required as it is about recording your wishes.

Question:

Where do I want to live when I am elderly or experiencing ill-health and unable to manage in my own home

Advice and Guidance:

It is very important to be realistic in your planning for where you want to live. You do not have to accept the viewpoints of those around you or follow typical patterns of behaviour in this regard. If you own your own home, you may find that a family member or close friend is willing and able to take care of you in your own home. If this is the case, you need to work out how it is going to be paid for. Is a family member willing to look after you in return for free accommodation or do they require some payment from you at the time or following your death? If you still owe money on your mortgage, and are unable to make the mortgage payments, this can be more complicated. If you live in rented accommodation, your planning needs to take into account the ongoing payments to your landlord as well as any costs involved in your care.

The main choices to make initially are do I want to stay in my own home or would I prefer to move into some other type of accommodation? If you wish to stay in your own home, you need to make it very clear in your planning if there are any circumstances at all in which you would be willing or comfortable moving out of your home and into other types of accommodation. For example, do you wish to stay in your own home until you die no matter what, or would you be willing to live in a hospice should you experience a terminal illness? Due to the requirement for executors to follow your wishes as recorded in legal documents, it is important to have thought through each scenario to its logical conclusion.

When you are thinking about issues of safety and security, you may be only thinking about your safety and security or your wish to leave your home to your spouse or partner or children, whereas another person may be more concerned about feeling safe and secure as they become more frail. For people concerned with safety and security as they age, it may simply be a question of acquiring more home security or having a dog. However, for other people it may seem more sensible to move into a group home or accommodation where security is present 24/7.

If you are thinking that you would prefer to move on to another type of accommodation, it is a good idea to go and visit a variety of types of accommodation run by a number of different service providers. It may be that you have particular views (such as a faith or religion) or belong to a particular group, that means you have a preference for a particular service provider or a particular type of accommodation. However for other people, the medical care and/or the ability of the service provider to understand autism and provide an environment that is sensorially acceptable is the most important thing. Without actually visiting, you will be unable to evaluate whether you think you would feel comfortable in that other accommodation.

Other types of available accommodation are:

- owner occupied retirement villages
- rental units in retirement villages
- fee-for-service supported accommodation (may or may not provide medical care)
- dementia care units
- hospice environments

Question:

I do not cope with being close to other people. I never shared a house and prefer solitary time to social time. I am getting older and I know that I will probably need to move into some kind of aged care accommodation in the future. Are there things I can do to manage that transition well and cope in an aged care home, especially if I need to share living space with others?

Advice and Guidance:

One thing which determines whether a difficult experience is manageable - such as moving into shared accommodation - is the attitude you have when you are approaching the change and when it has occurred. The fact that you are thinking about this and are prepared for a possible move into aged care accommodation is a good thing. There is a psychological skill called radical acceptance which is relevant here. Radical acceptance is all about being aware of a difficult situation and accepting what has happened or is inevitable.

The next step in the process of acceptance is to work out what the difficulty has taught you and how you are going to manage it. The opposite of radical acceptance is denial and regret. Even the most challenging situations can be managed through effective application of radical acceptance. It is not an easy skill and may require practice but as your attitude drives your emotions and experience of a situation, it will most likely provide some support around moving into aged care accommodation. If you try to avoid thinking and talking about moving into aged care then the opposite will most likely be true and can signal you are in denial which could mean you struggle with the move and new living arrangements, being driven by regret and name which will make your stay that much more unpleasant. Radical acceptance does not mean you are happy about the situation or that you give up. Rather it is about challenging your mind's negative view and worry and taking charge of the situation.

There are also some practical strategies around thinking about moving into aged care. It is advisable to research your choices. Some aged care accommodation is units or apartments which are self-contained. When someone needs more care, they move into the accommodation which offers staged medical care. Many people living in this sort of accommodation spend the majority of their time in their own units. It can be seen as very similar to independent living but with round the clock security and healthcare.

If you have to share space, especially your room, and are not yet good at it, try to learn to practice assertiveness. Being able to set boundaries is an essential part of sharing space and can make a big difference. Remember that neighbours in supported accommodation probably share some of your concerns and thoughts about shared living. Viewing them in this light rather than as frustrating, irritable, difficult or whatever else, may help you to make connections with your neighbours if you wish to. You can also talk to staff at the accommodation about your individual needs. While institutional or hospice care can seem disempowering, intimidating and monolithic, asserting your needs is really important. If you can, write down your preferences, information about autism as it relates to you and anything which triggers distress or meltdown.

Question:

I am terrified of death. I always have been. It gets worse as I get older. Are there ways that I can prepare myself and understand death better?

Advice and Guidance:

Death is a hard concept for most people to process and when we are thinking about our own death it is particularly hard. Some people have a religion / faith which gives them a sense of something beyond the grave but not everyone approaches the world that way. Many people are atheist or agnostic. And in fact, many people who have faith also fear death.

Some things which can help with fear of death include: Viewing your life as part of the cycle of nature and the universe can help. Taking the view that we are made from elements produced in stars which died counties millennia ago can give meaning and perspective for some people. Closer to home, we are the product of millions of years of evolution and when we die we go back into nature to support new life.

You can always think about your own legacy to the world. Thinking of things like your love or connections to those in your life – humans, animals or anything else you feel a strong connection with, the work you do, the support you give to others, the lessons you learn and wisdom you gather – these are all part of your legacy. Instead of worrying what you will leave behind try to focus on what you are doing while you are here. This kind of thinking can help address your fear of death.

Reflect on how many older people you know or know of who have reached the end of their life and are peaceful in death. At these times death is more like a blessing than a curse.

Reflect on the people you know who have died after serious illness. It would seem that the great majority of people when faced with expected death, make their peace and leave the world prepared and ready. While there are some exceptions to this, they do seem to be a small minority.

Think about the world before you were born. Reflect that if there is no afterlife, what you will experience when you die will simply be what it was like before you were born. This view enables you to see death as being like a sleep.

Focussing on making a difference while you are in the world can make life – and its end – more meaningful. Thinking about the impact you have on the world while you are here can help address some concerns around death, especially if you are concerned with your purpose and 'what it all means'.

Question:

When would I need to give power of attorney around my health and money to a family member and how does this work?

Advice and Guidance:

Power of attorney essentially means you assign the right to make decisions about your healthcare and / or finances should you become unable to do so.

The reasons people usually grant power of attorney is due to ageing and /or concerns about failing health. Financial power of attorney grants your chosen representative legal authority to act on your behalf for financial issues, Medical power of attorney designates the person who will make medical decisions for you in an emergency. You may wish to have separate documents relating to ageing and ill-health or you may wish to have one combined document. Where aspects are governed by power of attorney or any other legal framework where you reside it is a good idea to write down your wishes and plans prior to seeing a lawyer to have the legal paperwork drawn up. If you do not have your wishes and plans put into the legal paperwork by a lawyer; family members, service providers and other individuals may be able to challenge your wishes and plans in a court of law. This is particularly important in relation to issues that involve decision-making by next of kin where your chosen next of kin is not recognized in law and can be challenged by other family members.

Medical power of attorney can cover a range of decisions and often includes things like whether the person wants to be resuscitated in a number of situations. While laws around power of attorney are different in different countries, the process of appointing power of attorney for medical or finance decisions involves completing prepare forms and having these witnessed, signed and notarised by an adult.

This is not a thing to take lightly. It has resulted in people being defrauded by family members and taken advantage of in other ways. You don't want to find out the hard way that someone isn't trustworthy. While you can revoke a power of attorney arrangement hopefully you will not need to. Arrangements around power of attorney are usually done in consultation with family members. It is good to have a conversation about who would be willing to look after your health and finances who is not willing to do this for you. Preparation and consultation with a lawyer are useful in considering power of attorney decisions.

Question:

How do I remain independent as I age?

Advice and Guidance:

Independence can be a challenge for autistics at any age but entering into old age, this can pose even more difficulties, As autistics we are often treated with paternalism and have people thinking we need their 'help'. We tend to struggle with speaking up when something is wrong. Many autistic girls and women 'mask' socially, playing the part expected of them. This might be an effective strategy to avoid bullying or being ostracised, but it is not good for independence as it basically involves losing your sense of who you are, in order to be accepted by others. While perfectly understandable, it can come at the cost of identity and selfhood.

Older people face a degree of paternalism due to societal attitudes around ageing. This can occur in addition to disempowerment due to responses to autism by people in your life. There is a fine line between independence and risk for some older people. Authorities and family members may be concerned for your safety and recommend an older person moves from their home to an aged care home, and at times forcibly insist on this. For many autistic women an aged care home is probably at the very end of their list of preferred housing options. This is a complex area often with no clear-cut answers. Suffice to say staying independent as long as possible and practical is beneficial for both mental and physical health.

Some strategies for staying independent include:

- Maintaining or developing a strong sense of your identity, particularly your autistic identity. Knowing who you are and what you want is a good starting point for asserting your needs and wishing and also having strength and the will to look after yourself.

- Have meaningful activity in your life, whatever that may be for you.

- Have people in your life of all ages, where possible. This can include friends from the autistic community.

- Challenge yourself intellectually. This could include learning a language, doing difficult puzzles to other activities which make you feel your brain engaging i thought.

- Staying healthy; physically and mentally. This includes finding a doctor and specialists you respect and who respect and listen to you.

- Caring for others, such as grandchildren, can help maintain self-confidence and independence.

- Some older people stay in the paid workforce past retirement age. If you can, employment is a great way of maintaining your independence and self of self-worth. This does not need to be paid work and could be volunteering in the community.

▸ Living in a multi-generational household, whether within the main home or in a 'granny flat' or annexe. This can provide independence within the safety of your wider family.

CPSIA information can be obtained
at www.ICGtesting.com
Printed in the USA
FSHW021630081020
74519FS

9 781942 197577